Nancy Lake

Menus Made Easy

Nancy Lake

Menus Made Easy

ISBN/EAN: 9783742839541

Manufactured in Europe, USA, Canada, Australia, Japa

Cover: Foto ©Gila Hanssen / pixelio.de

Manufactured and distributed by brebook publishing software (www.brebook.com)

Nancy Lake

Menus Made Easy

MENUS MADE EASY;

OR,

HOW TO ORDER DINNER AND GIVE THE DISHES THEIR FRENCH NAMES

NANCY LAKE.

THE SIXTH EDITION.

LONDON AND NEW YORK:
FREDERICK WARNE & CO.
1891.

INTRODUCTION.

This publication is a humble endeavour to afford some assistance to ladies in the daily difficulty of what to order for dinner, and how to describe it.

Cooks are not generally gifted with fertile imaginations, and are inclined to get into a routine which is a source of annoyance to those who desire a variety of dishes, if not for themselves, at least for their friends. Ladies often wish to be ready with suggestions of a change in the proposals of the cook, and even when in some measure provided with these, a second difficulty arises—what are these dishes to be called? What are the correct technical names for them?

The French of cookery is a language of itself, and those who are not learned in it are often entirely at a loss when suddenly called on to write out a correct French menu with no other assistance than that of a dictionary. In carrying out this idea, lists of various dishes have been given, arranged in courses, with the French names, as well as the English equivalent or description.

It is not intended to give recipes, such as would be adequate for the preparation of the dishes in the kitchen; the dishes are only so far described as to enable the mistress to recognize them, giving a general idea of their ingredients and of their appearance when sent to table.

If the full recipes are desired for the cook's use, they will be found in the well-known cookery books, so many of which are now published.

CONTENTS.

	PAGE
INTRODUCTION	V

CHAPTER I.
SOUPS—Clear and thick 1

CHAPTER II.
FISH—Different modes of dressing Fish; Shell-Fish . . 10

CHAPTER III.
ENTRÉES—Of Beef, Veal, Mutton, Lamb, Pork, Poultry, Game 34

CHAPTER IV.
REMOVES—Of Beef, Veal, Mutton, Lamb, Pork, Poultry, Game 85

CHAPTER V.
ROASTS 111

CHAPTER VI.

Vegetables and Salads 114

CHAPTER VII.

Eggs and Omelettes 133

CHAPTER VIII.

Entremets — Cakes and Pastry, Puddings, Fritters, Compotes of Fruit, Creams, Jellies . . 138

CHAPTER IX.

Savoury Entremets 166

CHAPTER X.

Ices 172

CHAPTER XI.

Sauces and Garnishes 175

Fish.

Jean Doré *à la crémière* is boiled in milk and water, and served with a sauce of cream, butter and lemon-juice.

—— *à la purée de crevettes*—served in a purée of prawns, with melted butter and Béchamel sauce.

—— *à la batelière*—served in white sauce with button onions, mushrooms and essence of anchovy.

—— *en matelote marinière*—served in Matelote sauce with oysters.

—— *au gratin* is dressed in the same way as turbot.

LAMPREY.

Lamproie *à l'Italienne* is filleted, and stewed in wine with oil, onions, herbs and lemon-juice.

—— *au suprême* is cut up, sauté, and served in a sauce of red wine with truffles.

They are also dressed in many of the ways given for eels.

MACKEREL.

Maquereaux *à l'eau de sel* are boiled.

—— *à la maître d'hôtel*—broiled, and served in Maître d'hôtel sauce. Fillets are also dressed in this way.

Maquereaux *à la Flamande*—stuffed with chopped shallots and chives, butter, and lemon-juice; and broiled.

—— *grillés au beurre noir*—grilled, and served with black-butter sauce.

—— *aux groseilles vertes*—stuffed with green gooseberries, pieces of herring, &c.; boiled, and served in green gooseberry sauce.

Filets de maquereaux à la Vénitienne — fillets served in brown sauce with tarragon, chervil, truffles and port wine.

RED MULLET.

Rougets *en caisse* are broiled in papers, sprinkled with chopped parsley and oil.

—— *en papillotes* are baked in papers and served with Italian sauce.

—— *à la Ravigote*—baked in papers and served in Ravigote sauce.

—— *aux fines herbes*—cooked with butter, wine, Harvey sauce and anchovy. Served in the sauce with chopped mushrooms, parsley, shallot, and lemon-juice.

—— *à la maître d'hôtel*—served in Maître d'hôtel sauce. They are dressed in this way in fillets.

Filets de rougets à la Montesquieu — fillets cut in halves, sauté in butter with wine, lemon-juice, &c., and served with a sauce of melted butter and milk.

GREY MULLET.

Mulets *au beurre fondu* are broiled, and served with melted-butter sauce.

—— *grillés au vert*—broiled, and served with green sauce.

PERCH.

Perches are dressed in the same way as carp, tench and trout; and also in a water souché.

PIKE.

Brochet *farci* is stuffed and baked.

—— *sauce au beurre d'anchois*—boiled, and served with anchovy sauce.

—— *au bleu*—pickled.

—— *sauce raifort* — served with horse-radish sauce.

—— *sauce aux câpres*—served with caper sauce.

—— *en matelote*—stuffed and baked; served with Matelote sauce.

PILCHARDS.

Pélamides are dressed in the ways suggested for herrings.

PLAICE.

Plie *au gratin* are baked in brown sauce, covered with breadcrumbs. They are dressed in the same way as soles.

SALMON.

Saumon *à la tartare* is grilled, and served with Tartare sauce.

—— *à l'Écossaise* is crimped and boiled.

—— *à l'Indienne*—cut in pieces and stewed in curry sauce.

—— *à la Hollandaise*—served with Hollandaise sauce.

—— *à la Beyrout*—slices broiled in papers, and served in a sauce of onions, mushrooms, &c.

—— *à la crème d'anchois*—slices served in a sauce of melted butter, anchovy, &c.

—— *à la Cardinal*—a whole fish stuffed with fish forcemeat, braised, and served in Cardinal sauce.

—— *à la Régence*—a small fish covered with forcemeat, to which chopped truffles are added; served in Périgueux sauce.

—— *en matelote*—served in Matelote sauce.

Tranche, or *Darne, de saumon grillée*—a grilled slice of salmon.

Filets de saumon à l'Indienne — fried fillets, served with curry sauce.

—— *à la Maréchale* — fillets sauté, and served with Ravigote or Aurora sauce, garnished with shrimps or oysters.

—— *à la Tartare* — fried fillets, served with Tartare sauce.

—— *à la Ravigote* — fillets sauté, and served in Ravigote sauce.

Mazarine de saumon is a steamed mould of salmon forcemeat. It may be garnished with prawns, or served with Cardinal sauce.

Mayonnaise de saumon — pieces of cold salmon, with lettuce or other salad, and Mayonnaise sauce.

SHAD.

Alose *à la Maître d'hôtel* is baked, and served with Maître d'hôtel sauce. It is also dressed in fillets, sauté.

SKATE.

Raie *à la Maître d'hôtel* is served with Maître d'hôtel sauce.

—— *au beurre noir* — crimped and boiled; served with black-butter sauce.

—— *frite* — filleted and fried.

Raie *à la noisette*—filleted and boiled; served in butter sauce with the pounded liver of the skate, and Tarragon vinegar.

—— *aux fines herbes*—cooked with milk, butter, flour, lemon, herbs, &c., and served with fine-herbs sauce.

SMELTS.

Éperlans *à la Juive* are bread-crumbed, fried, and served without sauce. Served with anchovy sauce in a sauce-boat they are called *à l'Anglaise*.

—— *en ragoût*—stewed in white stock with herbs and wine.

—— *au gratin*—baked with melted butter and dried herbs, covered with breadcrumbs and sprinkled with wine.

Buisson d'éperlans—breadcrumbed and fried with their tails in their mouths. Melted butter should be served with them.

SOLES.

Soles *frites à l'Anglaise* are breadcrumbed and fried.

—— *au gratin*—covered with brown sauce and bread crumbs, and baked.

—— *à la Normande*—stewed with oysters, and baked with a rich brown sauce.

Fish.

Soles *à la crème d'anchois*—boiled and served in a sauce of white sauce and broth, with anchovy and whipped cream.

—— *à l'aurore*—stuffed and baked; served in a white sauce, with grated Parmesan and hard-boiled egg.

—— *à la Cardinal*—stuffed, baked, and served in Cardinal sauce.

—— *à la Colbert*—stuffed with Maître d'hôtel butter, and served with Maître d'hôtel sauce.

—— *à la maître d'hôtel*—served in Maître d'hôtel sauce. The same dish may be made with fillets.

—— *à la Trouville*—cut in two or three pieces, and cooked with butter, breadcrumbs, chopped onions, and cider.

Filets de soles au gratin—fillets breadcrumbed and fried; covered with brown sauce and breadcrumbs, and baked.

—— *à l'Italienne* are sauté, and served in white sauce, with wine, chopped shallots, &c.

—— *à la Hollandaise* are sauté, and served in Hollandaise sauce.

—— *en ravigote* are sauté, and served in Ravigote sauce.

—— *en matelote* are cut in halves, breadcrumbed, and fried; dressed in a crown, with Matelote sauce in the centre.

Filets de soles à la Rouennaise are coated with whiting forcemeat coloured with lobster spawn, and served with white Matelote sauce.

STURGEON.

Esturgeon *en fricandeau* is cut in thick slices, larded, stewed with bacon and mushrooms, and browned.

—— *à la Royale*—tied up in the form of a bolster, covered with forcemeat, and ornamented with pieces of truffle, tongue, &c.

Darne d'esturgeon au four is a baked slice of sturgeon.

—— *braisé* is larded and braised.

—— *grillé sauce piquante* is broiled, and served with Piquante sauce.

—— *à la bourguignotte* is served with Bourguignotte sauce.

TENCH.

Tanche *frite* is fried.

—— *sur le gril* is grilled.

—— *au court-bouillon*—boiled in court-bouillon, and served with caper sauce.

TROUT.

Truites *au bleu* are turned blue with boiling vinegar, and boiled in it with wine and vegetables; served with oil and vinegar.

—— *frites* are fried in butter.

—— *à la Beyrout*—served with Beyrout sauce.

—— *à la maître d'hôtel*—served with Maître d'hôtel sauce.

—— *à la Chambord*—cooked in marinade sauce, and garnished with crayfish, quenelles of fish, and sweetbreads.

—— *à la hussarde*—stuffed with butter and herbs; broiled, and served with Poivrade sauce.

Filets de truites à la Mazarine are fillets served in a sauce of melted butter, yolks of eggs, lobster spawn, anchovy, &c.

—— *à l'aurore* are covered with white sauce, grated Parmesan, and hard-boiled egg.

—— *à la Genevoise* are served with Genevoise sauce.

TUNNY.

Thon *frit* is cut in pieces and fried. It is served with Remoulade sauce.

TURBOT.

Turbot *à la Hollandaise* is served with Hollandaise sauce.

—— *sauce homard*—served with lobster sauce.

—— *à la crème*—served with a sauce of cream, yolks of eggs, and lemon juice.

—— *à la crème d'anchois*—served with a sauce of melted butter, anchovy butter, and cream, and sprinkled with chopped gherkins and capers.

—— *à la Mazarine*—served in the same sauce as fillets of trout "à la Mazarine."

—— *à la réligieuse* — served in Hollandaise sauce, sprinkled with chopped tarragon, and garnished with hard-boiled egg.

—— *grillé à la Vatel*—grilled; served with mussel sauce and crayfish.

—— *au gratin*, or *à la Béchamel*—pieces of turbot in Béchamel sauce, covered with breadcrumbs and grated Parmesan, and browned.

Turbot à la crème gratiné—alternate layers of pieces of turbot and of a sauce of milk, butter, flour, yolks of eggs, parsley, &c., sprinkled with breadcrumbs and grated Parmesan, and browned.

—— *au gratin à la Provençale*—alternate layers of pieces of turbot and Provençale sauce, breadcrumbed and browned.

—— *à la Parisienne*—stuffed and baked; served with a white sauce.

—— *à la Normande*—stuffed and baked; served with white Matelote sauce.

Petit Turbot à la Meunière is a small fish crimped, grilled, and served in a sauce of melted butter, yolks of eggs, and lemon juice.

WEAVERS.

Vives *au gratin* are stewed, breadcrumbed, and baked.

—— *à la Normande*—larded with pieces of eel and anchovy; cooked in wine with butter and vegetables, and served in the sauce. If served with Italian sauce they are called *à la Bordelaise*.

—— *à la Maître d'hôtel*—broiled and served with Maître d'hôtel sauce.

WHITEBAIT.

Blanchailles are fried. They should be served with lemon, cayenne, and slices of bread and butter.

—— *à la Diable* are devilled.

WHITING.

Merlans *au gratin* are breadcrumbed and fried with their tails in their mouths.

—— *à la Française*—dipped in milk, floured and fried. Served with anchovy or any other sauce.

Filets de merlans à la Hollandaise — fillets served with Hollandaise sauce.

—— *à l'Italienne* are served with Italian sauce.

—— *à la Orly* are floured, fried, and served with tomato sauce.

WHITING POLLOCK.

Colin *frit* is cut in slices, fried, and served with oil and lemon.

SHELL FISH.

CRAB.

Coquille de crabe is scalloped crab, served in the shell. It can also be dressed in a salad in the same manner as lobster.

CRAYFISH.

Écrevisses *au court-bouillon* are boiled in court-bouillon. If served in Bordelaise sauce they are called *à la Bordelaise*.

Aspic d'écrevisses — a mould of crayfish, meat jelly, and vegetables cut in shapes. Served with Mayonnaise sauce.

Petits pâtés aux écrevisses—covered patties, filled with crayfish and quenelles of fish.

Langouste *à la broche.* Sea crayfish roasted.

LOBSTER.

Homard *au court-bouillon* is boiled in court-bouillon and served with lobster sauce.

—— *à la Bordelaise*—cut up and served in Bordelaise sauce.

—— *au kari* — curried; served with boiled rice.

—— *en aspic*—slices coated with white sauce, in a mould of aspic.

Côtelettes de homard are lobster cutlets. They may be served with Mayonnaise sauce.

Miroton de homard à la Cardinal—slices of lobster, half of them dipped in white sauce, and half in the same sauce coloured with lobster butter. Dressed on a salad with Mayonnaise sauce.

Coquille de homard—scalloped lobster, served in the shell.

Croquettes de homard are croquettes of lobster with the coral and spawn, white sauce, yolks of eggs, &c., breadcrumbed and fried.

Rissoles de homard—the same preparation folded in a thin piece of paste, breadcrumbed and fried.

Petits vol-au-vents de homard are little puff paste patties filled with the croquette preparation of lobster.

Bouchées de homard à la Béchamel are patties smaller than the vol-au-vents, filled with chopped lobster in Béchamel sauce.

Petits pâtés de homard à la patissière are little covered lobster patties.

Mayonnaise de homard—the lobster cut up and served with lettuces and Mayonnaise sauce; ornamented with anchovies, olives, and pieces of hard-boiled eggs.

Salade de homard à l'Indienne — cut in slices and served on à salad with Indian pickles and Mayonnaise sauce; garnished with hard-boiled egg.

MUSSELS.

Moules *à la poulette* are cooked in butter with chives and parsley, and served in the sauce with yolks of eggs.

—— *à la Villeroi* are masked with Villeroi sauce; breadcrumbed and fried.

—— *au gras*—stewed with bacon, stock, flour, mushrooms, &c.

Coquilles de moules—scalloped ; served in scallop-shells.

OYSTERS.

Huîtres *à la Villeroi*—large oysters, each coated with Villeroi sauce, breadcrumbed and fried.

—— *au Parmesan*—browned with breadcrumbs, grated Parmesan, chopped parsley, and wine.

—— *en papillotes*—rolled in oval-shaped pieces of a paste made of mashed potatoes, flour and butter, and baked.

—— *à la Diable* are devilled—broiled, seasoned with butter, lemon-juice and cayenne. Slices of brown bread and butter are served with them.

Ragoût aux huîtres — stewed with vegetables, butter, flour, &c. Served in the sauce with yolks of eggs.

Coquilles aux huîtres—scalloped and served in scallop-shells.

Bouchées aux huîtres are small oyster patties.

Petits pains aux huîtres—oysters stewed with breadcrumbs and butter, and baked in very small rolls, from which the crumb has been scooped out.

Kromeskys aux huîtres — oysters cut up and cooked with butter, flour, yolk of egg, &c. Small pieces are wrapped in thin slices of bacon, dipped in batter and fried.

Croûtes aux huîtres—oysters pounded with cream and spread on small pieces of toast.

Andouillettes aux huîtres are small sausages of beef suet, breadcrumbs and oysters, with eggs, &c.

Croquettes aux huîtres are croquettes of oysters with oyster sauce, yolks of eggs, cayenne, and lemon-juice. Breadcrumbed and fried.

Rissoles aux huîtres are made of the same preparation wrapped in a thin coating of paste, breadcrumbed and fried.

Oysters can also be curried, or fried in butter, or dressed in a vol-au-vent, or in an omelette.

*SHRIMPS AND PRAWNS

These are dressed in *Rissoles* or *Petits pâtés* in the same way as lobster. They are called *Rissoles* or *Petits pâtés, de crevettes*—of shrimps, *de chevrettes* —of prawns.

The preparations of shell fish are generally served as entrées. Lobster *en aspic* may be served in the second course instead of a dressed vegetable.

CHAPTER III.

ENTRÉES.

BEEF.

The fillet, or undercut of the sirloin, is the part most used in the preparation of entrées. It is dressed as :

Filet de bœuf *à la Française*—cut in slices and broiled; served on Maître d'hôtel butter, with fried potatoes.

—— *à la Châteaubriand*, or *Châteaubriand grillé*—thick slices broiled and served in Châteaubriand sauce, or in Périgueux sauce, with mushrooms.

—— *à l'Italienne*—thin, oval-shaped pieces, floured, fried, and served in Italian sauce.

Escalopes de filet de bœuf à la Réforme—thin slices, each laid between two slices of bacon; breadcrumbed, with chopped ham mixed with the crumbs, and fried. Served with Reform sauce.

—— *à la Nemours* — thin slices covered with forcemeat and slices of ham, put together in pairs, breadcrumbed and fried. Served with a white sauce.

Escalopes de filet de bœuf à l'Ostende are spread with a sauce of chopped onions, Ostend or other oysters, white sauce, &c.; put together in pairs, breadcrumbed and fried. Served with a brown sauce.

—— *piqués au chasseur* are larded, soaked in marinade, and braised. Dressed in a crown, with brown sauce and currant jelly.

Grenadine de filet de bœuf à la Financière—cut in slices, larded, cooked in mirepoix, and served in the sauce with Financière garnish.

Tournedos à la sauce poivrade—slices of cooked fillet dressed in a crown alternately with fried slices of bread of the same size. Poivrade sauce in the centre.

This may be served with olives, or French beans, instead of the Poivrade sauce; and would then be called *Tournedos aux olives*, or *aux haricots verts*.

Slices of the fillet served with Piquante, Hollandaise, or other sauce, are called after the sauce with which they are served.

Mironton de bœuf are slices of cooked beef in a sauce of onions, butter, gravy, flour, &c.; covered with breadcrumbs and baked.

Bœuf en saucissons — slices of beef spread with forcemeat, rolled to the shape of sausages, stewed, and served in the sauce.

Bouilli en matelote — slices of boiled beef in a sauce of stock, wine, onions, mushrooms, &c.

Entre-côtes de bœuf à la Bordelaise are thick slices of ribs of beef broiled and served in Bordelaise sauce, with pieces of beef marrow.

Moëlle de bœuf *à la Oily*—beef marrow cut in long pieces, dipped in batter and fried; served with tomato sauce in a sauce-boat.

Quenelles à la moëlle are quenelles of beef marrow with breadcrumbs, eggs, &c.

Bouchées à la moëlle are small patties filled with marrow, and a savoury sauce of cream, shallot, chives, &c.

Petites croustades à la moëlle are made of the same preparation put into little cases of fried bread; breadcrumbs strewed on the top, and browned.

Vol-au-vent d'amourettes à la crème is a vol-au-vent of beef tendons, with Béchamel sauce and mushrooms.

Palais de bœuf *à la Robert* — ox palates cut in round or oval pieces, and served with Robert sauce. This dish may be served with other sauces instead of Robert, changing the name accordingly.

—— *à la Lyonnaise*—cut in pieces, and served in onion sauce.

—— *à la Ravigote* — oval pieces, dipped in white sauce with shallot, parsley, &c., breadcrumbed and fried; served with Ravigote sauce.

—— *à la Vivandière* are dressed in the same way, but served in a brown sauce with onions, butter, port wine, &c.

—— *en papillotes* — oval pieces in white sauce with parsley and mushrooms, broiled in papers, and served with Italian sauce.

For *Croquettes de palais de bœuf*, the palates are cut in pieces, and rolled, with forcemeat in the centre of each. Dipped in batter and fried.

They are also dressed in a vol-au-vent, or, if preferred, in several small ones as *Petits vol-au-vents de palais de bœuf*

Ox-tongue is served as:

Langue de bœuf *au Parmesan*—slices cooked with stock, wine and grated Parmesan.

—— *en papillotes*—slices wrapped in papers with slices of bacon, and broiled.

Turban de langue de bœuf à l'Écarlate — oval slices cut from two tongues, one pickled red, the other fresh; dressed in a crown alternately, with tomato sauce.

—— *à la Macédoine* is dressed in the same manner, and served with a white Macédoine garnish in the centre, and white sauce.

Ox-tails are dressed as:

Queue de bœuf *en haricot*, cut in joints, stewed, and served in the sauce with onions, carrots and turnips cut in shapes.

—— *aux navets au brun* — stewed, and served with turnips cut into small balls, and brown sauce.

—— *à la jardinière* — served with brown sauce, stewed button onions, and carrots and turnips cut in small shapes.

—— *en kari* — curried, and served with boiled rice.

—— *à la Marseillaise* — the pieces masked with a purée of onions, breadcrumbed and fried; served in brown sauce with garlic.

VEAL.

Grenadins de veau are oval slices cut from the "noix," larded, braised and glazed. They are served *aux petites racines* with potatoes, carrots and turnips, and brown sauce; or with Poivrade, tomato or other sauce, and called after it.

Poupiettes de veau are slices cut from the fillet, spread with forcemeat, rolled, and stewed with stock and wine.

Crème de veau is made with part of the fillet. It is pounded with eggs, cream, &c. steamed in a mould, or in several small moulds, and served with Périgueux sauce.

Veal Cutlets are served as:

Côtelettes de veau *à la Russe* — fried, spread on one side with a preparation of horse-radish, and breadcrumbed with grated Parmesan mixed with the crumbs; served with thin tomato sauce.

—— *à la Maintenon* — coated with a sauce of mushrooms, ham, eggs, &c., and baked or grilled in papers.

—— *en papillotes* — soaked in oil with mushrooms, lemon juice, &c.; wrapped in papers and cooked in the seasoned oil.

—— *à la Drayton* — thickly coated with a rich brown sauce, breadcrumbed and sauté.

—— *à la sans façon* — breadcrumbed with chopped shallots and parsley mixed with the crumbs, broiled, and dressed round mashed potato

Côtelettes de veau *à la Financière*—larded, braised and glazed; served with Financière sauce.

— *aux champignons* — larded, braised and glazed; served with a purée of mushrooms. They are also served with tomato or Jardinière sauce, or with dressed cucumber or asparagus, and named after the sauce or garnish with which they are served.

— *à la Saint-Garat*—larded with bacon and tongue, and braised. Set in aspic ornamented with hard-boiled egg, truffles, &c., and cut out. Served cold.

— *à la Princesse* — braised in white stock, coated with Mayonnaise sauce, and served cold with salad and aspic jelly.

For *Escalopes écossaises* they are cut in thin slices, breadcrumbed and fried, arranged in a circle with alternate slices of fried bacon, and Piquante sauce.

The Tendons, or gristly part of the breast, cut in pieces, are dressed as:

Tendrons, or **Amourettes, de veau** *aux petits pois*, stewed with butter, flour, stock, peas, &c.

— *frits* are soaked in vinegar and water, and fried

Entrées of Veal.

Tendrons de veau *à la Poulette*—cooked in a white sauce with onions, mushrooms, &c.

—— *au blanc* or *Blanquette de veau* — cooked in a white sauce with onions and vinegar.

—— *à la noble dame* — small pieces coated with a white sauce, dipped in batter and fried. Dressed with fried watercress in the centre, and a sauce of cream and butter.

—— *aux épinards* — oval pieces, braised and glazed; served with dressed spinach.

—— *en kari* — curried; served with a slice of fried bacon between each piece, and with rice in the centre.

—— *en Mayonnaise*—served cold in Mayonnaise sauce, with onions and gherkins.

Calf's Head for an entrée is boned, boiled, and cut in pieces. It is dressed as:

Tête de veau *à la Sainte-Ménehould*—the pieces coated with a sauce of butter and flour, breadcrumbed, sprinkled with melted butter, and browned.

—— *en moule* — chopped, and baked in a mould in alternate layers with chopped ham.

—— *à la Financière*—served with Financière garnish.

Turban de tête de veau à la Maître d'hôtel—
    the pieces dressed in a crown, with white
    sauce and Maître d'hôtel butter.
—— *à la Hollandaise* is served with Dutch
    sauce; *à la poulette* in white sauce with
    mushrooms, onions, and yolks of eggs.

Calves' Brains are dressed as:

Cervelles de veau *à la Provençale*—cooked
    in stock with wine, oil, parsley, garlic,
    &c., and served in the sauce.
—— *à la Ravigote* — boiled, cut in slices and
    arranged in a circle, with Ravigote sauce.
—— *en caisse au gratin*—small slices with a
    white sauce, baked in paper cases, with
    breadcrumbs on the top.

Croquettes de cervelles—made into croquettes
    with breadcrumbs, milk, eggs, &c., bread-
    crumbed and fried.

Marinade de cervelles—fritters made of pieces
    of the brains soaked in vinegar, dipped in
    batter, and fried.
        They are also served with Matelote,
    black-butter or other sauce, and take their
    name from it.

Calves' Ears dressed as:

Oreilles de veau *aux champignons* are boiled
    and served in a brown sauce, with yolks
    of eggs and mushrooms.

Entrées of Veal.

Oreilles de veau *farcies*—stuffed with forcemeat, breadcrumbed and fried; served with gravy.

—— *en marinade* — cut in strips, steeped in vinegar, &c., dipped in batter and fried; served with tomato sauce.

Calf's Tongue as:

Langue de veau *sauce tomates* is larded, stewed, cut in two and served in tomato sauce.

—— *à la jardinière* — stewed in white stock, cut in oval slices, glazed, and served with a Jardinière garnish. It is also served with Mushroom, Ravigote, or Piquante sauce.

The Liver is dressed as:

Foie de veau *à l'Italienne*—slices cooked with oil, wine, bacon, mushrooms, &c., and served in the sauce.

For *Pain de foie de veau* it is pounded and steamed in a mould with eggs, chopped ham, &c.; served with thin brown sauce.

Calf's Kidney is served as:

Rognon de veau *sauté*—minced, and sauté with butter, wine, brown sauce, &c.

—— *en caisse* — small round slices in brown sauce with chopped shallots, mushrooms,

&c., baked in small paper cases, the tops sprinkled with breadcrumbs.

Calves' Feet, after being boiled for jellies, are dressed as entrées, in tomato, poulette, or other sauce; the dish is called:

Pieds de veau *aux tomates,* or according to the sauce.

—— *à la bourgeoise* are stewed with bacon, veal, carrots, onions, &c., and served in the sauce, with the vegetables and meats.

For *Pieds de veau en friture* or *en marinade* small pieces are steeped in vinegar and water, dipped in batter and fried.

Calf's Tail, cut in pieces and boiled, is served as:

Queue de veau *à la Ravigote*—in Ravigote sauce; or *à la poulette*—in white sauce with onions and mushrooms.

Sweetbreads are dressed as:

Ris-de-veau *à la Villeroi*—slices coated with Allemande sauce, breadcrumbed and fried; served with a white sauce and any dressed vegetable.

—— *à la poulette* — cooked with flour, butter, mushrooms, onions, &c.

—— *à l'Anglaise* — breadcrumbed and roasted; served with gravy.

Entrées of Veal.

Ris-de-veau *frits*—dipped in batter and fried; served with tomato sauce.

—— *à la Provençale*—braised in stock with bacon and garlic, and served in the sauce.

—— *à l'Espagnole*—larded, braised in stock with veal, bacon, onions, &c., and served in the sauce.

—— *à la Toulouse* are larded, braised, and served with a Toulouse garnish.

—— *en fricandeau*—larded, braised and glazed; served on a purée of spinach or tomato.

—— *piqués à la Turque*—larded, braised and glazed. Cut in halves and dressed on a border of forcemeat, with rice in the centre, and suprême sauce over the rice.

—— *piqués aux truffes*—larded, braised, and served with truffle sauce. Jardinière or Financière sauce, dressed peas or cucumber, may be substituted for the truffle sauce, altering the name according to the sauce or vegetable with which they are served.

—— *en bigarrure*—half of them larded, braised and glazed, and half breadcrumbed and roasted. Dressed alternately, and served with tomato sauce.

—— *à la Chinoise*—small sweetbreads larded and braised, set in little moulds of aspic, ornamented with hard-boiled eggs, beetroot, &c. Served cold, with rice in the centre of the dish.

Côtelettes de ris de veau are slices of sweetbread, breadcrumbed and fried; served with plain gravy or with a white sauce.

Escalopes de ris de veau au suprême are oval slices, sauté, and served with suprême sauce.

—— *à l'Indienne* are breadcrumbed and fried; served with Indian sauce.

—— *en caisse* are small round slices in brown sauce with chopped mushrooms, &c., baked in paper cases, sprinkled with breadcrumbs.

Blanquette de ris de veau aux truffes are round slices cooked with slices of truffles in white sauce, with cream and yolks of eggs. Garnished with fried croûtons of bread.

Petites croustades de ris de veau are little cases of paste filled with sweetbread cut in dice, and white sauce with chopped truffles or mushrooms.

Andouillettes de Troyes grillées are broiled veal sausages, made with mushrooms, truffles, eggs, &c.

Boudin de veau à la légumière is a mould ornamentally lined with vegetables and filled with veal forcemeat. Steamed, and served with thin brown sauce.

Boudin de veau à la Richelieu is a mould lined with chopped truffles and filled with veal forcemeat. Steamed, and served with Périgueux sauce. These boudins are also steamed in several small moulds, lined in the same manner.

Quenelles de veau à la purée de champignons are poached quenelles of veal forcemeat served with a purée of mushrooms. They are also served with brown or white sauce or with any dressed vegetable.

Petits pâtés à la bourgeoise are small patties filled with veal forcemeat.

MUTTON.

Côtelettes de mouton *sauce tomates* are grilled, and served with tomato sauce.

—— *à la jardinière* are served with stewed vegetables.

—— *à la Soubise* are stewed with stock, &c. Served with the sauce round, and thick Soubise sauce in the centre.

—— *à la Provençale* are covered with a sauce of onions, garlic, butter, eggs, &c., breadcrumbed, with grated Parmesan mixed with the crumbs, and browned. Served with fried potatoes.

Côtelettes de mouton *à la Vicomtesse* are coated with a sauce of ham, mushrooms, yolks of eggs, stock, &c.; breadcrumbed and fried; served with paper frills round the bones.

—— *à la Bohémienne*—soaked in marinade, breadcrumbed and broiled; served with a sauce of some of the marinade with tomato and brown sauce, currant jelly, &c.

—— *en robe de chambre*—covered with forcemeat of veal, breadcrumbed and browned. Served with gravy.

—— *à la financière*—braised, and served with Financière garnish.

—— *braisées aux navets*—larded, braised, and dipped in aspic with Poivrade sauce; served cold with dressed turnips and broken aspic.

—— *à la Marquise*—a slice of ham laid on each cutlet, and veal forcemeat spread on it in a mound. Sprinkled with bread crumbs and browned. Served in white sauce with chopped ham.

—— *à la Réforme*—breadcrumbed, with chopped ham mixed with the crumbs, fried, and served with Réforme sauce. They may have a Réforme garnish in the centre.

Côtelettes de mouton *à la Marseillaise* —covered with an onion sauce, breadcrumbed and browned; served with Soubise sauce.

—— *à la Durcelle*—put into long paper cases, three in each, and baked in brown sauce with Harvey sauce, chopped onions, mushrooms, &c.

—— *panées grillées*—breadcrumbed and broiled, and served with plain gravy.

—— *aux pointes d'asperges*—served with a garnish in the centre of asparagus in white sauce with yolks of eggs, cream, &c.

—— *aux truffes*—served in brown sauce, with truffles cut in slices.

—— *aux petites racines*—on a mashed potato border with carrots and turnips cut in long shapes, and brown sauce. They are also served with any kind of dressed vegetable or purée of vegetable, or with Hollandaise, Italienne, Lyonnaise, Maître d'hôtel or other sauce. They are named after the sauce or vegetable with which they are served.

For *Chaudfroid de côtelettes à l'aspic* they are spread with forcemeat in a mound; coated with brown sauce, and served cold on a border of the forcemeat, garnished with aspic.

Turban de côtelettes de mouton à la Fermière

—they are dipped in Maître d'hôtel sauce with cream, and served cold, dressed in a crown with a salad of beetroot, cucumber and lettuce in the centre. *À la Palestine* they are served with Jerusalem artichokes cut into little balls, and white sauce.

Côtelettes à la Prince de Galles are pieces of stewed breast of mutton, breadcrumbed and fried; served with a purée of turnips, and gravy.

Ragoût de mouton à l'Irlandaise is Irish stew.

Haricot de mouton is haricot mutton. It is now often called *Navarin de mouton*.

Filets de mouton *au chevreuil*—the fillet or under part of the loin, cut in four parts, larded, and soaked in vinegar with vegetables, &c. Braised and served with Chevreuil sauce and French beans. Dressed in this manner it is also served *à la Macédoine*, with a Macédoine garnish in the centre, and brown sauce.

—— *à la minute* is cooked in stock with bacon, and served in the sauce.

The chump end of the loin, cut in thin slices, is dressed as *Escalopes de mouton aux fines herbes*, cooked with butter, flour, stock, chopped mushrooms, &c. Served with a garnish of fried croûtons, or sippits, of bread.

Carbonade de mouton (see Removes) is dressed as an entrée, cut in slices and served with Piquante, Poivrade or other sauce. The slices are also dipped in Maître d'hôtel sauce with cream, and served cold with a salad in the centre, as *Carbonade de mouton à la Fermière.*

Filets de mouton à l'Indienne are thick slices of roast mutton in a sauce of broth with chopped onion and curry paste; served with rice.

Petits pâtés de mouton à la Windsor are small covered patties filled with minced mutton, brown sauce, chopped mushrooms, &c.

Kidneys dressed as:

Rognons de mouton *à l'épicurienne* are cut open, breadcrumbed and broiled. The hollows filled with Tartare sauce; and devil sauce round.

—— *à la brochette* are dressed in the same way, the hollow of the kidneys filled with a lump of maître d'hôtel butter.

—— *à la Vénitienne*—cut in halves, fried in butter with chopped shallots, and dressed on a border. Brown sauce with anchovy butter, &c.

—— *au vin de Champagne*—thin slices served in a sauce of white stock, champagne or other white wine, flour and mushrooms, &c.

Rognons de mouton *en ragoût*—thin slices cooked in butter, with wine, flour, chopped mushrooms, shallot, &c.

Petits pâtés aux rognons—slices in white sauce put into little patties.

Sheep's Tongues are served as:

Langues de mouton *braisées*—larded, braised and served in the sauce with capers.

Cervelles de mouton *en caisse* are Sheep's Brains cut in small pieces, with Béchamel sauce, baked in little soufflé cases, the tops sprinkled with breadcrumbs.

Queues de mouton *au riz* are braised Sheep's Tails, coated with rice, breadcrumbed and fried. They are also served *au Parmesan*, omitting the rice and mixing grated Parmesan with the breadcrumbs.

Sheep's Trotters, though rarely seen at a gentleman's table in England, are much more often served in France. Boiled and cut in pieces, they are dressed as:

Pieds de mouton *en marinade*, soaked in marinade, dipped in batter and fried, and served with tomato sauce; or *à la Robert*, served in Robert sauce.

Pieds de mouton à la poulette are served with poulette sauce in a baked shape of rice.

LAMB.

Lamb Cutlets are dressed in most of the ways which have been suggested for mutton cutlets. There are also:

Côtelettes d'agneau *à la Princesse*—coated with Allemande sauce, breadcrumbed and fried. Served with white sauce, and dressed asparagus in the centre. For the cold entrée of this name the cutlets are sauté and served in Mayonnaise sauce.

—— *à la Duchesse*—coated with Duxelles sauce, breadcrumbed and fried. Dressed on a high vegetable border, with vegetables in the centre, and white sauce.

—— *à la boulangère*—dipped in oil and then in flour; broiled, and served with a sauce of cream, butter, &c.

—— *à la Robert*—breadcrumbed, broiled and glazed; served with Robert sauce.

—— *aux petits légumes*—breadcrumbed and fried; served with carrots and turnips, cut in long shapes, in the centre, and brown sauce.

Côtelettes d'agneau *au Parmesan*—dipped in a white sauce with grated Parmesan, breadcrumbed and fried.

—— *à la Pompadour*—coated with a mixture of chopped bacon, veal, truffles, &c., and served in papers.

—— *farcies aux truffes*—larded, coated with a purée of truffles; breadcrumbed and fried. Served with brown sauce.

They are also dressed in the same manner, using a purée of artichokes, asparagus, mushrooms, or turnips, instead of truffles; altering the name accordingly.

—— *en belle vue*—larded with tongue, ham or truffles, and braised. Set in aspic and cut out. Served cold with Mayonnaise sauce, or a Jardinière garnish.

—— *à l'aspic*—cutlets from a larded and roasted neck of lamb; coated with Provençale sauce, and served cold with aspic.

Épigramme d'agneau à l'ancienne is made of cutlets cut from a boned breast of lamb, an end of bone stuck in each, breadcrumbed and fried; arranged alternately with sauté neck cutlets. Served with small round slices of lamb in the centre, with mushrooms, and white sauce with cream, &c.

It is also served *aux concombres* with a garnish in the centre of dressed cucumber, or with any other vegetable, naming it accordingly.

Tendrons d'agneau aux pointes d'asperges — a braised breast of lamb cut up and arranged in a crown alternately with fried slices of bread, with dressed asparagus in the centre.

Blanquette d'agneau — small round slices of lamb and of ham or tongue, with white sauce, parsley, &c. It is served in a baked shape of rice; or in a croustade, or fried shape, of bread. Lamb is also dressed in *Croquettes* or *Rissoles*.

Lambs' feet are dressed *en marinade* and *à la poulette*, in the same manner as sheep's feet. As *Casserole de riz aux pieds d'agneau* they are served in a casserole, or baked shape, of rice. Lambs' tails are dressed in the same way.

Pieds d'agneau farcis are stuffed; served in Hollandaise sauce with chopped gherkins.

Queues d'agneau à la crémière are Lambs' tails served in white sauce with whipped cream, &c.

Lambs' Brains as *Cervelles d'agneau à l'innocent* are cut in thin slices and put in paper cases with white sauce, chopped parsley, &c. Sprinkled with breadcrumbs and browned.

Lambs' Ears are stewed and served as:

Oreilles d'agneau *farcies*, filled with a stuffing of veal forcemeat, &c., breadcrumbed and fried; served on a border, with Italian sauce.

—— *à la Ravigote* are served on a forcemeat border, with Ravigote sauce.

—— *à la Marquise*—served on a border with a peeled plover's egg in each ear. White sauce with cream, cock's combs, mushrooms, &c., in the centre.

Langues d'agneau *à la Persane* are stewed lambs' tongues, cut in halves and dressed in a circle, covered with a white sauce with wine, mushrooms, &c.; sprinkled with breadcrumbs and baked. Served with white sauce.

Lambs' Sweetbreads are dressed as:

Ris d'agneau *à la jardinière*, larded, braised and glazed. Served on a border with Jardinière sauce in the centre.

Dressed in this way they are served *aux petits pois, aux concombres, aux pointes d'asperges*, &c., with dressed peas, cucumber, asparagus or other vegetable in the centre, instead of Jardinière sauce.

Casserole de riz aux ris d'agneau — sweetbreads and cock's combs with Allemande sauce, in a baked shape of rice.

They may also be dressed in many of the ways suggested for *ris de veau*.

PORK.

Pork Cutlets are sauté, broiled, or breadcrumbed and fried. They are served with Robert, Tomato, Ravigote, Piquante, Indienne, or Rémoulade sauce, and called *Côtelettes de porc frais sauce tomates*, or *à la Robert*, according to the sauce with which they are served.

Dressed *à la Bolognaise*, they are breadcrumbed with grated Parmesan mixed with the crumbs, and fried. Served with brown sauce, and a garnish in the centre of short pieces of macaroni, mushrooms and tongue, with tomato sauce and grated cheese.

Small fillets from the under part of the loin, breadcrumbed and broiled, are called *Filets de porc à la Maréchale*.

Filets de porc *à la Hanovérienne* are larded, braised and glazed; dressed in a crown with white pickled cabbage in the centre, and brown sauce.

Dressed in this way they are served *aux épinards* or *aux pommes*, with spinach or apple sauce in the centre instead of the cabbage.

Escalopes de porc à la Lyonnaise are fillets cut in oval slices, breadcrumbed and fried.

Dressed in a border, covered with Soubise sauce, sprinkled with breadcrumbs and browned.

Escalopes de porc à la Robert are breadcrumbed and fried, and served with Robert sauce.

—— *à l'Indienne*—with Indian sauce.

Pig's Ears dressed as:

Oreilles de porc *à la Ste. Ménehould* are breadcrumbed and baked, and served with Rémoulade sauce.

—— *braisées* are braised and served in the stock, on dressed spinach.

—— *à la Lyonnaise*—cut in strips and cooked in stock with slices of onion, &c.

Pigs' Feet are dressed *en marinade* in the same way as sheep's feet; and as:

Pieds de porc *à la Ste. Ménehould*—pickled, breadcrumbed and fried.

POULTRY.

A very large number of dishes can be made with chickens, and they are, perhaps, more useful than anything else in the preparation of entrées.

Cut in joints they are dressed in the following ways:—

Poulets *à la tartare*—breadcrumbed and broiled; served with tartare sauce and pickles.

Entrées of Poultry.

Poulets *à la bonne femme*—stewed and served in white sauce.

—— *au chasseur*—soaked in oil with onion, &c., breadcrumbed and broiled; served in "Vin de Madère" sauce with chopped ham.

—— *à la Chabert*—cooked in oil with tomatoes, chopped parsley, garlic, &c.

—— *à la Marengo*—cooked in oil, and served in Italian sauce with the oil in which it was cooked.

—— *en kari* is curried, and served with rice.

—— *à la Orly*—the joints are floured and fried, and served in tomato sauce with slices of onion, which are also floured and fried.

—— *à la Provençale*—covered with a white sauce with slices of onion, garlic, &c.; sprinkled with breadcrumbs and browned.

—— *en marinade*—soaked in vinegar with herbs, &c., and fried in batter.

—— *sauté*—the joints are sauté, and served in a sauce of stock, wine, chopped mushrooms, &c.

—— *sauté aux truffes*—sauté, and served in brown sauce with truffles.

Fricassée de poulet — cooked in a white sauce with mushrooms, cock's combs, pieces of sweetbread, &c.

—— *à l'ancienne*—cooked with flour, butter, milk, young onions, &c.

For *Fritot de poulet*, the joints are soaked in oil with onions, &c., dipped in flour and fried. Served with tomato sauce.

Fillets of fowl, or fat pullet, are dressed as:

Filets de volaille, or **poulardes**, *au suprême*, on a border, covered with Suprême sauce.

— *aux champignons* — covered with white sauce with cream and mushrooms. If slices of truffles are substituted for the mushrooms, the dish is called *aux truffes* instead of *aux champignons*.

— *à la Duchesse* — half the fillets larded, braised and glazed, and half sauté; dressed alternately in a crown, with cock's combs in the centre, and white sauce with cream, &c.

— *à la Talma* — the larger fillets larded, braised and glazed, the small under fillets stuck with pieces of French beans and sauté. Arranged in a circle, with dressed spinach in the centre, and brown sauce.

— *à l'Ambassadrice* — cut in slices, and coated with forcemeat of fowl with chopped truffles. Breadcrumbed, half of them with chopped truffles, and half with chopped ham mixed with the crumbs;

sauté, and arranged alternately. A purée of cucumbers with cream in the centre.

Filets de volaille *à la Dumas*—each one divided in two, masked with a purée of cucumbers with white sauce, &c, bread-crumbed and fried; served on a purée of cucumbers with cream.

—— *à la Nesselrode*—masked with a white sauce with cream, &c., and served cold, dressed alternately with glazed slices of tongue on a border of hard-boiled eggs; a salad in the centre with Mayonnaise sauce.

—— *aux concombres* are arranged in a circle alternately with stewed pieces of cucumber; served with a purée of cucumber.

—— *aux pointes d'asperges* are coated with Suprême sauce, and dressed alternately with pieces of tongue of the same size; asparagus points in the centre.

Suprême de volaille is the same dish served with Suprême sauce, and with truffles instead of asparagus in the centre. It may be served cold as *Chaudfroid de filets de volaille au suprême.*

For *Suprême de volaille à la Royale* the fillets are dressed on an ornamental border of vegetables, with a macédoine garnish in the centre, and a small piece of truffle or tongue on each fillet.

Sauté de filets de volaille à la Cardinal is composed of sauté fillets arranged in a circle with alternate slices of truffle; Cardinal sauce in the centre.

Poulet à la Princesse is a cold entrée prepared with fillets of chickens cut in oval slices, coated with a sauce of aspic and cream, set in aspic and cut out; served on an aspic border, with salad.

Salade de filets de volaille à la Brunow—small round slices of fowl and slices of cucumber stewed with white sauce, aspic and peas. Cut in square pieces, and dressed on a salad border, with white tartare sauce.

Blanc de volaille aux concombres — slices from the breast of a roast fowl, with pieces of cucumber, white sauce, cream, &c.

Côtelettes de volaille à la Dauphine are made with the legs of fowls from which the thigh-bone has been removed. They are dipped in Allemande sauce, breadcrumbed and fried. Served with a dressed vegetable in the centre and white sauce.

Legs of fowl are also boned, stuffed with forcemeat, and served as *Cuisses de volaille*, or *poulardes, à la jardinière*, with a Jardinière garnish; *aux concombres* or *aux petits pois*, with dressed cucumber or peas.

Entrées of Poultry. 63

Cuisses de volaille *au soleil* are stuffed with forcemeat, larded in rays, braised, and served on a pyramid of forcemeat, with mushroom sauce.

—— *à l'écaillère* are stuffed with forcemeat and oysters, and dressed on a pyramid of forcemeat, with oyster sauce.

—— *truffées à la Périgord*—the thigh-bone removed, they are stuffed with truffles and maître d'hôtel butter, and braised; served in a crown with paper frills round the bones, and with truffle sauce.

—— *à la Bayonnaise*—the thigh-bone removed, they are cooked in oil with onions, and served in a white sauce, sprinkled with breadcrumbs and browned.

—— *farcies aux petits légumes* are boned, stuffed and braised. Dressed on a border, with carrots and turnips cut in shapes, and brown sauce.

Chaudfroid de volaille — cooked fowls cut in pieces, coated with white sauce and white meat jelly. Served cold, dressed in a circle with alternate slices of tongue.

—— *en mayonnaise*—the pieces are coated with Béchamel sauce and served cold on a salad with Mayonnaise sauce, or with aspic whisked to a froth with Tarragon vinegar and oil.

Mayonnaise de volaille—pieces of fowl served on a salad, covered with Mayonnaise sauce and garnished with olives, anchovies, &c.

Chaudfroid de fricassée is a fowl cut up and coated with a white sauce. Served cold, garnished with aspic.

Capolitade de volaille—pieces of fowls served in Italian sauce with capers, or in brown sauce with wine; garnished with croûtons of fried bread.

Chartreuse de volaille is an ornamental mould of mixed vegetables, with pieces of chicken in the centre.

Crème de volaille—a purée of fowl with cream, steamed in a mould garnished with truffles, tongue, &c.

Petits soufflés de volaille are made of a purée of fowl and beaten eggs; baked in little soufflé cases.

Soufflé glacé de volaille—minced chicken soaked in oil, vinegar, &c.; put into a soufflé dish in alternate layers with aspic whipped to a froth, and iced.

Moule d'aspic à la Royale is prepared with small round slices of fowl, slices of truffle, mushrooms and cock's combs, with Béchamel sauce and aspic. Cut into oval pieces and dressed in a mould of aspic, ornamented with hard-boiled white of egg and truffles.

Small puff paste patties filled with minced chicken and white sauce, with tongue, mushrooms or truffles, are served as *Petites bouchées*, or *Petits pâtés, à la Reine*.

Bordure de riz à la Reine is a round wall of rice filled with minced, or purée of, fowl. It is sometimes garnished with plovers' eggs round the edge.

Minced chicken, with ham or tongue, can be made into *croquettes*, breadcrumbed and fried, or into *rissoles*, folded in thin paste and fried. The latter are sometimes coated with broken vermicelli.

Croquettes de volaille aux truffes are made with chopped truffles instead of ham or tongue, and are served with truffle sauce. Dressed with tongue and served in a white sauce with chopped tongue they are called *Croquettes de volaille à l'écarlate*.

Quenelles de volaille are quenelles of chicken forcemeat. They are poached and served with a dressed vegetable, or dipped in white sauce, breadcrumbed and fried.

—— *au Suprême* are poached, and dressed in a circle with Suprême sauce, and a vegetable in the centre.

—— *en demi deuil* are poached, and half of them rolled in chopped truffles. Dressed in a crown, with white sauce and chopped truffles.

Quenelles de volaille à l'écarlate are dressed in a crown alternately with glazed slices of tongue of the same size, and served with Suprême sauce. If a Russian tongue is used they are called *à la Russe* instead of *à l'écarlate*.

Boudins de volaille à la Lucullus are quenelles of chicken forcemeat with a piece of purée of truffles in the centre of each; served in a croustade, or shape of fried bread, with Allemande sauce.

—— *à la Richelieu* are oblong pieces of quenelle forcemeat, dressed in a crown with Périgueux sauce.

Cigarettes à la Reine are made of chicken forcemeat with white sauce and chopped truffles. Pieces the shape of cigars, breadcrumbed and fried.

Rissolettes de volaille à la Pompadour are diamond-shaped sandwiches of the preparation for chicken croquettes with truffles, between layers of chicken forcemeat. Dipped in batter and fried.

Ravioles à la Napolitaine are little pieces of chicken or game forcemeat wrapped in paste. Arranged in a circle with alternate slices of Parmesan cheese; baked, and served with brown sauce.

Timbale de Nouilles is a mould lined with paste, filled with German paste, minced chicken, grated cheese, &c.

—— *à la Champenoise* is filled with minced chicken, anchovies, gherkins, truffles, &c., with white sauce and wine.

Foie gras à l'aspic is a mould of aspic with pieces of foie gras in it.

Foie gras can also be dressed with truffles in little patties, as *Petits pâtés à la Montglas;* or larded with pieces of truffle, braised, and served with truffle sauce as *Foie gras à la Périgueux.*

DUCKS.

The fillets of roast ducks are served as:

Filets de canetons *aux petits pois* — in a circle, with stewed peas in the centre; *à la Macédoine,* with a vegetable Macédoine in the centre; or *à la Bigarade,* with Bigarade sauce.

—— *farcis* — a boned duck covered with forcemeat of fowl, cut in pieces the shape of fillets, and dressed in a crown with a vegetable garnish in the centre.

Caneton *à la Diable* is a roast duck cut up and devilled—served in a sauce of wine, catsup, mustard, cayenne, &c.

The legs of roast ducks, in a sauce of stock and wine with shallots, &c., are served as *Salmis de cuisses de canetons*.

GOOSE.

The legs of a roast goose are cut in pieces, fried with slices of onion, and served with Piquante sauce as *Quartiers*, or *cuisses*, *d'oie à la Lyonnaise*.

TURKEY.

The pinions of a turkey as:

Ailerons de dindon, or **dinde**, *à la purée de céleris* are boned, and served in a circle with a purée of celery in the centre.

—— *à la Ste. Ménehould* are boiled in stock with wine, &c., coated with the sauce, breadcrumbed and broiled.

Escalopes de dinde en blanquette, or *Blanquette de dinde*, are slices cut from the breast of a roast turkey, served in white sauce with cream, &c. With the addition of slices of ham it is called *au jambon*.

Slices of the breast are also served as:

Émincé de dinde à l'Italienne, with slices of gherkins and Italian sauce.

Abatis de dinde à la Chipolata are the giblets stewed and served with Chipolata garnish.

PIGEONS.

Fillets of pigeons are served as:

Filets de pigeons *à la Duxelle*—coated with Duxelle sauce, breadcrumbed and fried. Served with Provençale sauce and mushrooms.

Côtelettes de pigeons *au fumet de gibier*—breadcrumbed and fried, and a small piece of bone stuck in each to imitate cutlet bones. Dressed in a crown with fumet of game sauce.

—— *à la Parisienne*—stuffed with forcemeat, breadcrumbed and fried. Dressed in a crown with alternate fried croûtons of bread, and a brown purée of cucumbers in the centre. This dish may be served *à l'Italienne* with Italian sauce, or with any vegetable garnish, instead of the purée of cucumbers.

Pigeons are also cut in halves and boned, with the exception of the leg bones. They are stuffed, breadcrumbed and broiled, and served as *Côtelettes de pigeons à la Financière*, in a circle, with a Financière garnish in the centre.

GAME.

VENISON.

Hachis de venaison is hashed venison.

Venison Cutlets, sauté and dressed in a crown, are served as:

Côtelettes de venaison *aux olives*, with a sauce of port wine, brown sauce, olives, &c.

—— *aux champignons*—with brown sauce and mushrooms.

—— *au jus de groseilles*—with Poivrade sauce and red currant jelly.

Rouelles de cerf à la St. Hubert are slices of fillet of venison, larded and cooked in brown sauce with wine, slices of gherkins, &c.

Civet de chevreuil is jugged roebuck.

Côtelettes de chevreuil *sautées* are cutlets of roebuck cooked in butter with wine, stock, mushrooms, &c., and served in the sauce.

—— *sautées sauce Poivrade* are sauté, and served in Poivrade sauce with pickled mushrooms.

Côtelettes de chevreuil à la Bohémienne are soaked in marinade, breadcrumbed and broiled. Served in brown sauce with some of the marinade, currant jelly, &c.

Slices from any joint are served in Piquante sauce with currant jelly, &c., as *Émincé de chevreuil.*

HARE.

Civet de lièvre is jugged hare.

Lièvre, or **lévraut,** *sauté*—a hare cut in pieces, sauté, and served in a sauce of broth and wine with mushrooms, &c.

Filets de lièvre, or **lévraut,** are fillets of hare fried and dressed in a circle with a brown sauce. They are also *piqués*—larded and braised, and served with Poivrade sauce. Served with tomato sauce they are called *piqués sauce tomates.*

—— *piqués à la Bourguignotte*—cut in halves, larded and braised. Dressed in a crown with a brown sauce, bacon cut in dice, young onions, &c.

Côtelettes de lièvre à la Dauphine are slices cut from the fillets with a small piece of bone stuck in each, breadcrumbed and fried. Arranged in a crown with Piquante sauce and chopped olives.

Turban de lièvre à la Péronne—fillets dressed in the same way, and arranged in a circle alternately with quenelles of forcemeat of hare. White sauce with vinegar, pickled onions, &c.

Boudins de lièvre—rolls of forcemeat of hare, breadcrumbed and browned.

RABBITS.

Cut in joints, Rabbits are served as:

Lapereau, or **Lapin**, *sauté aux fines herbes*—sauté, and served in fine-herbs sauce.

—— *sauté aux truffes*—with brown sauce and slices of truffles; or *aux olives*, substituting olives for the truffles.

—— *à la Vénitienne*—larded, braised in oil and wine with veal and garlic, and served with the sauce.

—— *en kari*—curried and served with rice.

—— *en gibelotte*—stewed with onions, bacon, wine, &c.; served in the sauce with mushrooms.

—— *en papillote*—boned, coated with a stuffing of bacon, mushrooms, &c., and broiled in papers.

The backbone with the fillets, cut in sections, larded and braised, is served as *Grenadins de* **lapin** or *lapereau*, with brown sauce and spinach.

Côtelettes de lapereau à la Soubise are made with the legs cut in two, boned—but a small piece of bone stuck in each piece. Spread with forcemeat and served with Soubise sauce.

Filets de lapereaux *aux concombres* are fillets of roast rabbits in a white sauce with slices of cucumber.

—— *à la Valenciennes* are cut in halves and dressed in a crown with white sauce, cream and mushrooms. Dressed in this way with alternate pieces of ham, they are called *à l'écarlate*.

They are also served *à la Musulmane*—larded and braised. Dressed in a crown with curry sauce, and rice in the centre.

Turban de lapereau à la Douarière is composed of fillets cut in two, half of them larded and braised, and half sauté. Arranged alternately, with quenelles of forcemeat of rabbit in the centre, and brown sauce with wine, &c.

Lapereau en salade — fillets of roast rabbits soaked in oil and vinegar; served cold on a salad, garnished with hard-boiled egg, beet-root, &c.

Escalopes de lapereau au fumet—fillets cut in oval slices, and arranged alternately with slices of truffle; covered with a white sauce made of rabbit, and baked. *Aux pointes d'asperges* the slices are served in a white sauce with asparagus.

For *Fricassée de lapereau* the rabbit is cut up and cooked in a white sauce with wine, mushrooms, &c.

Boudins de lapin are made of a poached roll of rabbit forcemeat. Served with mushrooms or truffles, in brown sauce. It is also cut in pieces and dressed on a border.

—— *à la Richelieu* — a roll of forcemeat of fowl, truffles, &c., thickly covered with forcemeat of rabbit, breadcrumbed and broiled. Served with Périgueux sauce.

Purée de lapereau bordure de riz is a purée of rabbits in a border of rice.

Timbales de semoule au chasseur are small moulds of semolina, breadcrumbed and fried, filled with forcemeat of rabbit and purée of mushrooms.

Many of the ways in which chickens are dressed are also suitable for rabbits.

PHEASANT.

A roast pheasant, cut up, is served with Salmis sauce and mushrooms or truffles, as *Salmis de faisan*.

Faisan *au velouté de gibier* is served in a white game sauce; *à la purée de gibier* in a purée of game.

—— *à la bonne femme* is cooked with square pieces of ham, slices of Portugal onions, &c.

Fillets of pheasants are served as:

Filets de faisans *piqués aux légumes*—larded and braised. Dressed in a crown alternately with stewed pieces of cucumber of the same size. Jardinière garnish in the centre.

—— *à la Comte de Brabant*—larded and braised. Arranged alternately with slices of bacon round a pyramid of Brussels sprouts. Fumet of game sauce.

—— *à la marquise*—half of them larded and braised, and half breadcrumbed and fried. Arranged alternately, with white game sauce, and white cock's combs in the centre.

—— *à la Maintenon*—cut in halves and coated with a white sauce with chopped mushrooms, &c.; broiled in papers, and served with gravy.

Chaudfroid de filets de faisans is a cold entrée of fillets of roast pheasants cut in halves, coated with a game sauce, and garnished with hard-boiled eggs.

Galantine de faisan aux truffes is a pheasant boned, and stuffed with game forcemeat, rabbit, truffles, &c. Braised, and served cold with a garnish of aspic.

Boudins de faisan à la Richelieu are oval-shaped pieces of forcemeat of pheasant, breadcrumbed and fried. Served with Richelieu sauce.

Quenelles of forcemeat of pheasant, dressed in a crown with game sauce and mushrooms or truffles, are called *Turban de quenelles de faisan*.

PARTRIDGE.

Roast partridges, cut up, are served as *Salmis de chasseur* in a sauce of oil, wine, lemon, &c.

As *Salmis chaudfroid de perdreaux*, the joints are masked with Salmis sauce and aspic jelly. Served cold with a garnish of aspic.

Fillets of roast birds, as *Filets de perdreaux aux petits legumes*, are dressed in a crown, with young onions, carrots and turnips cut in shapes, and game sauce.

Côtelettes de perdreaux *à la Bacchante* are fillets with a piece of bone stuck in each, breadcrumbed and fried. Served in a white game sauce with raisins, juice of grapes, &c. They are also served *à la*

Douarière, with quenelles of forcemeat of partridge in the centre, and game sauce.

Épigramme de perdreaux aux champignons is composed of fillets, half of them sauté, and half larded and braised. Arranged in a crown, and served with game sauce and mushrooms.

For *Épigramme de perdreaux à la Périgord* the fillets are dressed alternately with quenelles of forcemeat of partridge. Served with chopped truffles in a game sauce.

Escalopes (thin round or oval slices) cut from the fillets, are served as *Perdreaux en escalopes*, or *Sauté de perdreaux*, in a white game sauce with mushrooms, &c. If truffles are substituted for the mushrooms, the dish may be called *Sauté de perdreaux aux truffes*.

Chartreuse de perdreaux is an ornamental mould of vegetables filled with larded and braised partridges, pieces of sausage, dice of bacon, &c.

Pain de perdreaux is a purée of partridge steamed in a mould; served with brown game sauce.

Perdreaux en soufflé or *Omelette soufflée de perdreaux*, is made of a purée of roast partridges with eggs, &c., and is baked in a soufflé dish or in small paper cases.

GROUSE.

Roast grouse, cut up, are dressed as:

Grouse *à la Ailsa* — covered with fumet of game sauce with yolks of eggs, &c., sprinkled with breadcrumbs and browned.

—— *à la Commodore*—the joints coated with forcemeat of grouse, and dressed in a pyramid with a rich game sauce.

For *Salmis de grouse aux truffes* they are served in fumet of game sauce with slices of truffles; garnished with croûtons.

Salade aux grouses—the joints masked with salmis sauce and aspic. Dressed on a salad with Mayonnaise sauce, garnished with hard-boiled eggs, &c.

The fillets are served as *Filets de grouse à la chancelière*, dressed in a crown, with small quenelles of veal in the centre, and game sauce.

Black-game and Ptarmigan are dressed like grouse.

WILD DUCK.

Roast wild ducks, cut up, are served as:

Canards, or **Canetons, sauvages** *en salmis* with a salmis sauce.

Canards sauvages à la bigarade—with bigarade sauce.

The fillets as—

Filets de canetons sauvages *au fumet de gibier* are served in a crown with fumet of game sauce.

—— *à l'essence*—served with a brown game sauce, port wine, shallots, &c.

—— *à la Syrienne* — dressed alternately with slices of fried bread spread in a dome shape with the livers with butter, &c. Served with brown game sauce and olives.

TEAL.

Teal are dressed in the same way as wild ducks; also as:

Sarcelles *à la purée de champignons*—cut in joints and arranged in a circle with a purée of mushrooms in the centre; served with a macédoine garnish they are called *à la macédoine de légumes.*

Filets de sarcelles aux anchois are fillets of teal with stock and grated Parmesan, a fillet of anchovy laid on each, sprinkled with breadcrumbs and Parmesan, and browned.

Turban de filets de sarcelles à la Toulouse— fillets dressed in a crown, with fumet of game sauce, pickled mushrooms, &c.

Turban de filets de sarcelles à la moderne—the fillets are spread with forcemeat of game, and served with a fumet of game sauce.

WOODCOCKS.

Salmis de bécasses—the birds cut up and served in salmis, or fumet of game, sauce.

—— *au chasseur*—served in a game sauce, with wine, mushrooms, &c. The insides are spread on croûtons, and arranged round the dish.

Turban de bécasses aux champignons—the birds cut in halves and dressed in a crown, with game sauce and mushrooms.

Chaudfroid de bécasses—the joints masked with brown game sauce, and brown meat jelly; served cold.

Filets de bécasses *à la Lucullus*—fillets coated with forcemeat and served on a border of toasted bread, with a thick purée of woodcocks piled in the centre, and game sauce round.

—— *à la Talleyrand* are dressed in a crown, with the insides spread on croûtons of fried bread of the same size as the fillets. Fumet of game sauce with truffles.

—— *en canapé* are laid on slices of crust of bread. A stuffing of the trail with bacon, &c., piled on the top. Served with a game sauce.

Croustade de bécasses à la Comtesse is a low oval croustade, or shape of fried bread, filled with a purée of woodcocks; the fillets dressed on the top alternately with cock's combs.

SNIPES.

Snipes are dressed in the same way as woodcocks, but are cut in halves where woodcocks are filleted. They are also served as:

Bécassines *à la bonne bouche*, filled with a forcemeat of foie gras and bacon; dressed on a forcemeat border, covered with forcemeat and baked. Served with truffle sauce.

QUAILS.

Cailles *aux laitues* are braised, and served with stewed lettuces.

—— *aux petits pois* are served with peas cooked in white stock.

—— *aux truffes* are stuffed with the livers, truffle, &c., and are served with Périgueux sauce.

Turban de cailles à la Financière—roast quails cut in halves and dressed on a border, with

Financière garnish in the centre. It is also served *aux concombres*, with stewed pieces of cucumber, and a purée of cucumbers in the centre.

For a *compote de cailles* they are cooked in wine and stock with slices of sweetbread, ham, truffles, &c.; garnished with croûtons. They are also dressed in a vol-au-vent with Toulouse garnish, as *Vol-au-vent de cailles*.

PLOVERS.

Plovers can be dressed in any of the ways that are suggested for woodcocks. The fillets of roast birds are served as:

Filets de pluviers *aux champignons*—in a circle alternately with croûtons spread with the trail; game sauce with mushrooms.

LARKS.

A salmis of larks is called *Mauviettes en salmis*.

Mauviettes *grillées* are broiled; served on slices of fried bread.

—— *à la chipolata* are cooked with Chipolata garnish.

—— *en caisse* are boned, stuffed with forcemeat and baked in paper cases.

For a *Turban de mauviettes à la Parisienne* the larks are boned, stuffed with game forcemeat and truffles, and braised; dressed in a crown, with small quenelles of veal in the centre, and a game sauce. Dressed alternately with large quenelles of game forcemeat, they are called *aux quenelles*.

Mauviettes *en côtelettes* are boned, spread with forcemeat and served with brown sauce.

They are also dressed as:

Croustade de mauviettes — boned, stuffed, and baked in a croustade of fried bread with Périgueux sauce and mushrooms.

Vol-au-vent de mauviettes — boned, stuffed, and served in vol-au-vent case with white game sauce and mushrooms.

ORTOLANS.

Ortolans *à la Périgourdine* are served in truffles, of which the centres have been cut out.

— — *en caisse* are baked in small paper cases with Périgueux sauce.

Crème de gibier is a purée of game, steamed in a mould, or in several small moulds.

Petites bouchées de gibier are little patties of game.

—— *à la purée de gibier* are little patties filled with purée of game.

Petits pâtés au jus are little patties lined with forcemeat, and filled with gravy.

Kromeskis à la Russe are made with pieces of any kind of forcemeat or croquette preparation, wrapped in slices of bacon, dipped in batter and fried.

Cassolettes de riz are patties of rice paste, breadcrumbed and fried; filled with forcemeat or croquette preparation.

Timbales à la Pahlen are small moulds lined with macaroni, filled with a white forcemeat—veal or fowl—and a black forcemeat of truffles, &c., in the centre.

Timbale à la Milanaise is Milanaise garnish in a shell of paste.

CHAPTER IV.

REMOVES OR RELEVÉS.

BEEF.

A ROAST sirloin of beef is called *Aloyau à la broche.*

For *Aloyau de bœuf à la Provençale* the sirloin is larded and spread with a stuffing of marrow, anchovies, garlic, &c.; roasted, and served with Piquante sauce.

The upper part of the sirloin, boned and rolled, is served as:

Aloyau *braisé à la royale*—larded and braised.

—— *à la Printanière*—braised and served with young vegetables.

—— *à la Portugaise*—larded and braised; served with stewed Portugal onions and brown sauce.

—— *à la Godard*—braised, and served with slices of sweetbread, mushrooms, &c.

The fillet, or undercut of the sirloin, is usually cut out and dressed as a separate dish.

It is roasted and served as *Filet de bœuf rôti*, and may have a vegetable garnish—Macédoine, Jardinière, or Printanière—and be named accordingly. *Au jus d'orange* it has orange sauce.

Filet de bœuf *au macaroni* is garnished with macaroni.

—— *à la Napolitaine*—larded, soaked in oil with vegetables, &c., roasted, and served with Neapolitan sauce.

—— *au jus de groseilles*—larded, soaked in marinade and roasted; served with a brown sauce, currant jelly, &c.

—— *piqué aux légumes printaniers*—larded, roasted and glazed; served with young vegetables and brown sauce.

—— *à la Milanaise*—larded, roasted, and served in white sauce with macaroni, &c.

—— *à la Bohémienne* — larded, soaked in marinade, and roasted or braised. Served with fried slices of potatoes and Poivrade sauce with pickled onions, pickled mushrooms, and olives; or cold, with tomato sauce, currant jelly, &c.

Braised, it is served as *Filet de bœuf braisé*; *à a sauce Madère* it has Madeira sauce.

A Round of beef is served as:

Rouelle de bœuf—*bouillie*, boiled; *au four*, spiced, and baked in water with suet.

The Brisket as:

Pièce de bœuf *garnie à la Flamande* is braised and garnished "à la Flamande."

Noix de bœuf *braisée* is a braised chump of beef.

Ribs of beef rolled and braised are served as:

Côtes de bœuf *braisées à la purée de tomates*, with a purée of tomatoes in the sauce; or *à la Milanaise*, with macaroni instead of the tomato purée.

—— *aux racines* are larded and served with carrots; *à la Portugaise*, with Portugal onions.

Pièce de bœuf à la St. Florentin is a rolled loin served with Robert sauce.

Beef or Rump Steak as:

Bifteck *à la Française* is broiled, and served with fried potatoes.

—— *en ragoût* is stewed.

It is also boiled in stock, and served with a Flamande garnish as *Pièce de bœuf bouillie à la Flamande*. Garnished with sausages, bacon and cabbages, it is *garni de choux*. As *Bœuf bouilli à la Macédoine de légumes* it is served with a Macédoine garnish.

Rosbif *à l'Anglaise* is roast beef, served with horseradish and Yorkshire pudding.

Bœuf braisé aux haricots verts is braised beef served with French beans.

Bœuf *Hollandaise* is a piece of beef rubbed with treacle, &c., salted, smoked and boiled. It is eaten cold.

Pâté de bœuf aux pommes de terre is a pie of minced beef and mashed potatoes, with a crust of mashed potatoes.

Pâté chaud d'escalopes de filet de bœuf is a hot pie of slices of fillet of beef, ham and potatoes, with brown sauce.

Ox-tongue, or *Langue de bœuf*, boiled and glazed, is served *à la prima donna* with a border round it of quenelles of veal, and white sauce with Brussels sprouts.

VEAL.

A Fillet of veal is dressed as:

Rouelle de veau *aux petits pois* — larded and roasted; served with peas in white sauce.

—— *à la Pontoise*—stuffed, roasted, and served cold with Tartare sauce.

—— *à la potagère*—larded and roasted; served with carrots cut in shapes, onions, cauliflower and brown sauce.

—— *à la jardinière*—stuffed with a piece of bacon, roasted, and served with a Jardinière garnish.

Rouelle de veau *à la Princesse*—stuffed with forcemeat, mushrooms, &c.; roasted, and served with slices of tongue and bacon, and white sauce with cream.

——— *à la Versaillienne*—stuffed with a tongue and forcemeat; roasted, and served with quenelles, slices of stewed cucumber and white sauce with cream, &c.

——— *en thon*—larded with fillets of anchovy, pickled, and cooked in oil.

A Chump of veal larded and braised is served as:

Noix de veau *à l'oseille*, or *aux épinards*, on a purée of sorrel or spinach; *à la bourgeoise* with brown sauce.

——— *à la potagère* is braised white, and served in a white sauce with peas and pieces of cauliflower.

It is also served *à la purée de champignons*, on a purée of mushrooms; or *aux petits légumes*, with stewed young carrots, turnips and onions, and brown sauce.

For *Veau en fricandeau*, veal is larded on one side with thick strips of bacon, on the other side with fine ones, and braised.

The Loin as:

Longe de veau is roasted. Served *à la Strasbourgienne*, it has slices of Strasbourg or other bacon round it, and Poivrade sauce.

It is served cold *au jambon*, with oval slices of ham and croûtons of aspic; or *à la dame blanche* with a sauce over it of Béchamel and aspic with Tarragon vinegar, &c., garnished with Indian pickles.

Larded and braised, it is served *piquée braisée;* or *à la macédoine de légumes*, with a vegetable macédoine. *À la Cambacères*, it has a border round it of small slices of tongue, truffles and cucumber; white sauce with wine, chopped mushrooms, &c.

The under part of a loin is roasted and dressed as *Filet de veau à la crèmière*, with poached eggs, and Béchamel sauce with cream, &c.

A Neck of veal dressed as:

Carré de veau *au naturel* is stewed, and served in the sauce with chopped gherkins and vinegar.

À la Milanaise, it is braised, and served with a Milanaise garnish.

Roasted, it is served *à la purée de céleris*, with stewed heads of celery and purée of celery sauce.

À la St. Clair, with slices of fried ham and tomato sauce.

À la Bruxellaise, with Brussels sprouts and white sauce.

A Breast of veal as:

Poitrine de veau *rôtie* is roasted, and served with brown sauce and melted butter; *à la Soubise*, with Soubise sauce.

Boned, stuffed, rolled and braised, it is served *à la printanière* with spring vegetables; or *à la Chipolata*, with Chipolata garnish.

Galantine de veau is served cold, garnished with aspic.

Calf's head is served as:

Tête de veau *au naturel*, stewed, and garnished with the tongue and brains.

—— *farcie* is stuffed with forcemeat, &c., and stewed.

—— *en tortue*—it is cut in pieces and boiled with vegetables and turtle herbs—basil, marjoram, thyme, bay leaves, &c. Served in the sauce with wine and mushrooms.

Veal and ham pie is called *Pâté de veau au jambon*.

Timbale à la Française is a pie of layers of slices of larded veal, ham and forcemeat, in a shell of paste.

Pâté de pieds de veau à l'Écossaise—a pie of calf's feet minced with suet and apples, with gravy and wine.

Pâté chaud de godiveau is a hot pie of veal or fowl forcemeat.

MUTTON.

Hanche de mouton is a roast haunch of mutton. It may be served *au jus de groseilles* with brown sauce, currant jelly, &c.

—— *à la Bohémienne* — soaked in marinade, roasted, and served in a brown sauce with pickled onions, olives, currant jelly, &c.

A leg or neck of mutton is also dressed in this way.

A fore-quarter of Southdown mutton is called *Quartier de pré-salé*; if served with haricot beans it is *à la Bretonne*.

A Saddle of mutton as:

Selle de mouton *à l'Anglaise* or *en broche* is roasted.

—— *au laver*—served with laver and a brown sauce.

—— *rôtie à la venaison*—it is hung a fortnight; roasted, and served in a brown sauce with wine, &c.

—— *à la Mirabeau*—roasted, and served in Poivrade sauce with chopped gherkins and beetroot.

—— *à la Polonaise*—the meat of a roast saddle is cut out, minced, and put back again with brown sauce, &c., keeping the shape by a wall of mashed potatoes. It is sprinkled with breadcrumbs, and browned. Dressed in this way, with a purée of onions over the mince, and served with Soubise sauce, it is called *à la Marseillaise*.

A Leg of mutton as:

Gigot *rôti* is roasted.

—— *à la Russe* — roasted, and the cooking finished in burning brandy. Served with the gravy and brandy.

—— *à la Provençale*—garlic inserted into the leg; roasted and served with Bretonne sauce.

—— *en chevreuil*—larded, soaked in oil and roasted. Served with Poivrade sauce.

Removes of Mutton.

Gigot *bouilli*—boiled; served with carrots and mashed turnips. It is also served with caper sauce—*sauce aux câpres*.

Larded and braised it is served *à la Jardinière*—with a Jardinière garnish; *à la Napolitaine*—with macaroni and Neapolitan sauce; *à la Soubise*—with Soubise sauce and potato croquettes.

—— *de sept heures* is boned, and stewed for seven hours with onions, carrots, &c.

—— *farci* is boned, stuffed and roasted. Served with tomato or Soubise sauce.

—— *braisé*—stuffed and braised.

—— *à la Bretonne* is stuffed and braised, and served with Bretonne sauce and haricot beans.

—— *à la Polonaise* is braised, cut in slices without severing them from the bone, and a stuffing put between each slice.

A Neck of mutton as:

Carré de mouton is roasted; *bouilli*, boiled and served with carrots and mashed turnips, and caper sauce in a sauce-boat.

—— *au riz*—cooked with rice, slices of onion and dice of ham.

—— *à l'Irlandaise* is braised and served with onions and potato croquettes.

—— *à la Jardinière*—with a Jardinière garnish;

or with any dressed vegetable or purée, naming it accordingly.

Carré de mouton *à la Provençale*—spread with a purée of onions, breadcrumbed and browned. Served in brown sauce with garlic.

—— *à la Soubise*—larded, braised, and served with Soubise sauce.

—— *au chevreuil*—larded, soaked in marinade and braised. Served with Chevreuil sauce and potatoes cut in little balls. If stewed prunes are substituted for the potatoes it may be called *à l'Allemande*.

—— *à l'Algérienne*—larded, soaked in marinade and roasted. Served in brown sauce with some of the marinade and French plums.

Carrés de mouton à la légumière are two necks roasted, put together like a saddle, and the space between filled up with mashed potato, garnished with other vegetables.

A **Loin** of mutton may be dressed in many of the ways suggested for necks. Also as:

Carbonade de mouton—boned, larded, and rolled with forcemeat in the centre; braised and glazed. Served with a dressed vegetable, Soubise or Piquante sauce, or *à la Nivernaise*, with stewed carrots.

A shoulder of mutton boned, stuffed, and roasted or braised, is served with Piquante sauce as *Épaule de mouton farcie*. *En ballon,* it is boned, larded, made into the shape of a balloon and braised.

A mutton pie made with potatoes and onions, covered with potato paste, is called *Pâté de mouton à l'Irlandaise.*

LAMB.

Hanche d'agneau is a roast haunch of lamb. It is sometimes called *Rosbif d'agneau à la broche.*

The Forequarter as:

Quartier d'agneau *à la broche,* is roasted.

—— *à l'hôtelière*—roasted and served in a sauce of maître d'hôtel butter with cream.

—— *farci*—a stuffing put between the neck and shoulder; roasted and served with brown sauce.

Côtes d'agneau *à la chancelière* is a roast forequarter, the shoulder cut out and the meat of it minced with ham, truffles, &c., and white sauce, put into the space the shoulder was cut from. Breadcrumbed, browned, and served with white sauce.

Selle d'agneau *rôtie* is a roast saddle of lamb. It is served *à l'Indienne,* with Indian sauce and Indian pickles; and *à la bonne fermière,* with lamb's fry breadcrumbed and fried, and a sauce of broth with chopped mint.

Selle d'agneau *braisée à l'Allemande*—boned, stuffed and braised; served with Allemande sauce and any vegetable garnish.

—— *à la Villeroi* is dressed in the same way, covered with Allemande sauce and sprinkled with breadcrumbs and grated Parmesan.

—— *à la Ménagère* is dressed in the same way as saddle of mutton *à la Polonaise*, with a white instead of a brown sauce, and the meat cut in small square slices.

A Leg of lamb is dressed in the same way as a leg of mutton. Also as:

Gigot d'agneau *bouilli aux épinards*, boiled and served on spinach; or *à la Palestine* with a purée of Jerusalem artichokes.

The Neck as:

Carré d'agneau *aux petits pois* is roasted and served with green peas; or *aux légumes printaniers* with spring vegetables.

—— *à la Bruxellaise* is braised and served on a purée of Brussels sprouts.

The Shoulder, or—

Epaule d'agneau, is roasted; served *à la maître d'hôtel*, with maître d'hôtel sauce; or *aux pointes d'asperges*, with asparagus heads and white sauce.

Boned, larded, braised and glazed, it is served as *glacée*.

—— *à la Montmorency*—boned, stuffed with forcemeat, larded and braised; served with

Toulouse garnish. It is also dressed *à la Polonaise* in the same way as a saddle of mutton.

Pâté chaud d'agneau is a hot pie of lamb cutlets with potatoes, white sauce, &c.

PORK.

Selle de porc frais is a roast saddle of pork. *À la Robert* it has Robert sauce.

A Leg of pork as—

Gigot de porc *bouilli* is boiled with the carrots, turnips and parsnips with which it is served.

—— *à la Piémontaise* is roasted and served in a brown sauce with Indian pickles, olives, &c.

—— *à l'Allemande* is pickled, boiled, and served with stewed red cabbage and pickled cabbage, carrots and turnips, and Poivrade sauce.

Échinée de porc rôtie is a roast chine of pork.

Carré de porc *à la Rémoulade*—a roast neck served in Rémoulade sauce with chopped Indian pickles.

Longe de porc *rôtie* is a loin roasted.

Pâté à la Leicestershire is a pork pie in a crust made with hog's lard instead of butter.

—— *à la Devonshire* is a pie of layers of slices of pork, bacon and apples.

Salt pork boiled with cabbages and other vegetables, and served with them, is called *Petit salé aux choux.*

A sucking pig is plainly roasted; or stuffed with truffles, &c., as *Cochon de lait à la Périgueux;* or with chestnut and sausage-meat stuffing, and served with Chipolata garnish, as *à la Chipolata.*

À la Savoyarde—stuffed with sausage-meat, rice, &c., and roasted; served with little sausages, and a white sauce with wine and mushrooms.

Cochon de lait en galantine is a braised galantine of sucking pig.

Pâté froid de cochon de lait is a cold sucking pig pie.

A Ham as:

Jambon *à la broche aux épinards* is roasted, and served with spinach. If a York ham is used, the dish is called *Jambon d'York à l'Anglaise.*

—— *à la Maillot* is braised in wine; served with vegetables and Madeira sauce.

—— *glacé à la Jardinière* is glazed, and garnished "à la Jardinière." It is also served *à la Macédoine, aux petits pois* or *aux haricots verts,* with a garnish of Macédoine, green peas or French beans.

Fromage de cochon is brawn.

A haunch of boar, or *Cuissot de sanglier,* may be served *à la Royale,* larded, and braised in wine and water with vegetables, &c., sprinkled with breadcrumbs and served with the sauce.

Filet de sanglier au chasseur is a fillet of boar,

soaked in oil, &c., and braised; served in the sauce with Poivrade sauce.

Hure de sanglier is a boar's head.

POULTRY.

A capon boiled in stock with bacon, onions, &c., is served in the sauce as *Chapon au gros sel*. Stuffed with truffles, &c., and roasted, it is served *à la Périgueux*, with Périgueux sauce; or *à la Piémontaise*, with tomato sauce and raviolis.

A fowl boiled and served with Bourgeoise sauce is called *Poule au pot*.

A fat pullet, or *poularde*, is roasted and served *à la financière* with Financière garnish; or *aux légumes printaniers* with stewed young vegetables and brown sauce.

À la Grimod de la Reynière it is filled with a stuffing of the liver with truffles, mushrooms, &c. Roasted in slices of bread and ham.

À la Montmorency it is larded, stuffed with foie gras, bacon, &c. Braised and glazed.

À la Guillaume Tell it is boned, stuffed and braised; set in a mould with the stock, garnished with truffles, and served cold.

For *Pilau de poularde* it is cooked with spice, onions, rice, &c. Masked with the rice, and garnished with hard-boiled eggs.

Poulets et langue are two boiled chickens with a tongue between them; white sauce with any vegetable garnish.

Poulet *au riz* is a chicken boiled with rice.

—— *à la Chivry* is cooked in mirepoix with slices of bacon, and served in Ravigote sauce.

—— *à la Mona*—cooked with wine, tomato sauce, Portugal onion and bacon.

—— *à la d'Escars*—larded, and braised in stock and wine with bacon, vegetables, &c.

—— *rôti à la peau de goret* has a crackly skin from melted lard having been dropped on it while roasting.

—— *à la Milanaise*—stuffed, roasted, and served with Milanaise garnish.

—— *à la Hambourgeoise*—stuffed with butter, chopped parsley, &c., and roasted.

—— *à l'estragon*—the stuffing is made of the liver, bacon, tarragon, &c. It is roasted, and served in a white sauce with chopped tarragon.

—— *à l'Italienne*—filled with a stuffing of the livers with bacon, mushrooms, &c. Roasted, and served in a white sauce with oil, wine, tarragon, &c.

—— *à la sauce tomates* is stuffed, braised, and served with tomato sauce.

Petits poulets *à l'Indienne* are young chickens stuffed with rice, breadcrumbs, curry powder, &c. Braised, and served with rice and Indian sauce, garnished with Indian pickles.

Petits poussins are very young chickens. They are larded and braised, and served *à la Vénitienne* in a white sauce with wine, cock's combs, chopped mushrooms, &c.; or *à la chevalière*, in white sauce with button onions, mushrooms, &c.

Pâté chaud de volaille au jambon is a hot chicken and ham pie.

—— *froid de volaille aux truffes* is a cold chicken pie, with forcemeat and truffles.

DUCKS.

Ducks are roasted and served *au jus d'orange*, with orange sauce; or braised and served *aux petits pois*, or *aux champignons*, with stewed peas or mushrooms.

Canards, or **canetons**, *au Père Douillet* are braised in wine and stock, and served in the sauce.

—— *à la St. Michel*—braised in wine and broth, and served with mushrooms, &c., in the sauce

—— *à l'Espagnole*—braised with vegetables, oil, and garlic; served in a brown sauce with olives.

—— *à purée verte* are stewed ducks, covered with a purée of green peas.

They are also served *aux navets, au céleri*, or *aux olives*, with stewed turnips or celery, or with olives.

GOOSE.

Oie *rôtie* is a roast goose, served with apple sauce in a sauce-boat.

—— *braisée à la Jardinière* is braised, and served with brown sauce and Jardinière garnish.

—— *à la Chipolata* — served with Chipolata sausages.

—— *rôtie, farcie de marrons*—stuffed with the liver, chestnuts, &c., and roasted.

—— *à la Portugaise*—stuffed with slices of Portugal onions, wine, &c., roasted, and served with stewed Portugal onions and a brown sauce.

—— *à l'Arlesienne*—stuffed with onions, truffles, chestnuts, &c., braised in mirepoix, and served in tomato sauce.

—— *en daube* is stuffed, braised, and served cold covered with the sauce.

Pâté aux abatis d'oie is giblet pie

TURKEY.

Dinde *rôtie* is a turkey roasted, and garnished with sausages.

—— *rôtie parfaite* is stuffed with sausage-meat, chestnuts and truffles, and roasted.

—— *à la purée de céleris* — boiled, and served

with a purée of celery and slices of fried bacon.

Dinde *à la Chipolata*—stuffed with sausage-meat and chestnuts, roasted, and served with Chipolata garnish.

―― *truffée*—stuffed with forcemeat and truffles; roasted, and served with gravy and chopped truffles.

―― *à la Provençale*—a stuffing of onions, bread-crumbs, &c.; roasted and served with truffle or tomato sauce.

―― *en daube*—larded and stewed; served cold, covered with the sauce.

―― *à la Yorkshire*—the legs are cut off, it is boned and stuffed with forcemeat and a tongue, and served with white sauce and vegetables.

A young turkey, roasted, is served as *Dindonneau à la duchesse*, with a purée of cucumbers, quenelles, small pieces of tongue, and French beans.

Galantine de dinde is a braised galantine of turkey; it is served cold.

―― *de dinde aux foies gras* has fat livers of fowls added to the forcemeat.

PIGEONS.

Pigeons stewed in stock with bacon, mushrooms, onions, &c., are served in the sauce as *Pigeons en compote*.

Pigeons *à la crapaudine* are breadcrumbed and broiled; served with Piquante sauce.

—— *en ragoût d'écrevisses* are stewed, and served in a white sauce with mushrooms and crayfish.

—— *aux petits pois* are stuffed, and stewed with onions, green peas, &c.

Pâté chaud de pigeons, or *pigeonneaux*, is a hot pigeon pie.

—— *de pigeons à l'Anglaise* is a pigeon pie with collops of beef steak.

GAME.

VENISON.

The haunch of venison, or **Hanche de venaison**, ranks first amongst removes.

Dressed *à la Corinthienne*, it is larded, soaked in marinade and roasted; served in a brown sauce with port wine, currants, currant jelly, &c.

Quartier de venaison is a fore-quarter of venison.

Gigot de cerf, or *venaison*, is a leg of venison.

Filet de cerf, or *venaison*, is a fillet of venison.

Épaule de cerf, or *venaison*, is a shoulder of venison.

Carré de cerf, or *venaison*, is a neck of venison.

The forequarter of a roebuck is served as *Quartier de chevreuil;* the leg, as *Gigot de chevreuil.*

A venison pasty is called *Pâté de venaison.*

HARE.

Lièvre, or **Lévraut,** *sauce Poivrade,* is larded, roasted, and served with Poivrade sauce.

—— *au jus de groseilles*—larded, roasted, and served in brown sauce with olives and currant jelly.

—— *rôtie à la Finnoise*—larded, roasted, and served in a sauce of stock, vinegar, sour cream, &c.

Râble de lièvre rôti is a baron of hare, larded and roasted.

Lièvre en daube is boned, and stewed in a jar with bacon, veal, game stock, &c. It is served cold, in the jar.

Pâté de lièvre à l'Écossaise is a pie of stewed hare with wine, &c.

Pain de lièvre à la Yorkshire is a pie of layers of slices of hare, ham and hard-boiled eggs, with game jelly. It is served cold.

RABBITS.

As *Lapereaux à l'Anglaise* they are stewed, and served with Soubise sauce.

Lapereaux *grillés* are flattened and broiled; served with butter and chopped-parsley.

—— *aux petits pois* are cooked in a white sauce with onions, green peas, &c. If mushrooms are substituted for the peas they are called *à la Tavernière*.

—— *à la Jardinière* are cooked in white sauce, with young onions, carrots and turnips cut in little balls, and peas.

—— *à la villageoise*—stuffed, roasted, and served in melted butter sauce with shallots, &c.

Galantine de lapins is made of rabbits boned without removing the heads. It is served cold, garnished with the sauce in which it is braised, in a jelly.

Rabbit pie is served as *Pâté chaud de lapereaux*.

PHEASANTS.

Faisans *à la Soubise* are braised pheasants covered with Soubise sauce; *aux marrons*, with chestnut sauce.

—— *à la purée de gibier* are larded, braised, and served with purée of game sauce.

—— *à la Fontainebleau*—the breasts are larded in a square. They are braised in white stock with lettuces, sausages, &c., and served with the lettuces and sausages, and brown sauce.

Faisans *à la Gitana*—stewed with bacon, slices of Portugal onions, tomatoes, wine, &c.

—— *à la Flamande*—stewed with bacon, sausages, cabbages, &c.; served with the cabbages pressed and cut in shapes, carrots and turnips, and Poivrade sauce.

—— *à l'étouffade*—larded and stewed; served with game sauce.

—— *aux foies gras*—stuffed with foie gras, ham, truffle, &c., and roasted.

—— *truffés à la Piémontaise* — stuffed with truffle stuffing, roasted, and served with a sauce of aspic and wine with slices of truffles.

—— *à la Bohémienne*— stuffed with foie gras, truffle, &c.; cooked in mirepoix, and served in the sauce with truffles and foie gras.

—— *à la Saint-Cloud*—boned, filled with a stuffing of the livers with partridge, truffles, &c.; roasted, and served on toast with Italian sauce and truffles.

Pâté chaud de faisan aux truffes is a pie of pheasant with forcemeat and truffles.

PARTRIDGES.

Partridges braised in stock with bacon, cabbages, &c., are served as *Perdreaux aux choux*, with the cabbages and slices of bacon.

Perdreaux *braisées* are larded and braised.

—— *à l'étouffade*—larded, and stewed in stock and wine with onions, &c.

—— *à la Parisienne*—cooked in a brown sauce with wine, and served in the sauce.

—— *à l'Anglaise*—stuffed with the livers and butter, and roasted. A stuffing of shallots, breadcrumbs, &c., is inserted under each joint, and they are served in a sauce of stock and wine.

—— *truffés à la Périgord*—stuffed with truffle stuffing and roasted; served in a white sauce with truffles.

—— *à la Mecklenbourg*—stuffed with chopped French plums, game forcemeat, &c.; cooked in stock and wine, and served in the sauce with tomato sauce and currant jelly.

—— *à la Victoria*—the breast bones removed, stuffed with game forcemeat, larded and braised; served with brown sauce, wine, &c.

Pâté de perdreaux au chasseur is a pie of partridges with veal and bacon, mushrooms, and onion sauce.

GROUSE.

Grouse are dressed like Pheasants *à la Piemon-*

taise. *À la Kinnaird* they are stuffed, roasted, and served with Financière garnish.

Pâté de grouse à l'Écossaise is a pie of grouse with beef steak, &c.

BLACK GAME.

As *Coqs noirs*, or *Coqs de bruyère, à la royale*, blackcocks are larded, braised, and served with a white sauce and little rissoles of game.

À la Rob Roy they are stuffed, roasted with sprigs of heather and whiskey, and served with melted-butter sauce.

Grouse are also dressed in this way.

SNIPES.

Snipes cut in halves, baked on layers of bacon, with butter, are served cold as *Bécassines en terrine à l'Irlandaise*.

Boudin de bécassines à l'épicurienne is composed of snipes, mushrooms, truffles, &c., with wine, in suet crust.

Quails, Plovers, and Larks may be dressed in hot pies, and served as *Pâté chaud de cailles, pluviers,* or *mauviettes;* or in cold pies, as *Pâtés froids*. Any small birds may be used for these pies.

Pâté de mauviettes à la Melton Mowbray is a lark pie with veal and bacon, mushrooms, truffles, &c.

Larks or other small birds are dressed as *Boudin à la Chipolata*, with Chipolata garnish in suet crust.

Pâté froid de gibier is a cold pie made of the meat of several kinds of game.

—— *à la Yorkshire* is composed of goose, hare, grouse and snipes, with spices, sausage meat and slices of ham.

CHAPTER V.

ROASTS, OR RÔTS.

Black Diver—*Macreuse.* Dressed *au chocolat* they are served covered with chocolate.

Black Game—*Coqs noirs,* or *Coqs de bruyère.*

À la Stockholm they are larded on one side, and barded with vine leaves on the other side.

Bustard—*Outarde canepetière.*

À la Russe they have a slice cut in the breast and a stuffing inserted, and are served with brown sauce.

Capon—*Chapon.* Served with watercress it is called *au cresson.*

Chicken—*Poulet.* Served *à la Forrester* it is covered with watercress leaves, mustard and cress, &c.

Bardé, it is barded—roasted with a slice of bacon over the breast, and served with the bacon on it.

Rôti à la Staël it has a white crust from being sprinkled with flour during the roasting.

Spring Chickens—*Petits Poulets.*

Young Chickens—*Petits Poussins.*

Duck—*Canard.*

Duckling—*Caneton.* Served with orange sauce it is called *au jus d'orange* or *à la bigarade.*

Goose—*Oie.*

Green Goose—*Oison* or *Oisillon.*

Grouse—*Grouse.*
À la bonnie lassie they are served on brown bread toast with melted-butter sauce.

Guinea Fowl—*Pintade* or *Gelinotte.*

Piquée they are larded; *bardée,* barded.

Hare—*Lièvre.*

Lapwings—*Vanneaux.*

Larks—*Mauviettes.*

Leveret—*Lévraut.*

Ortolans—*Ortolans.*

Partridges—*Perdrix* or *Perdreaux.* "Perdrix" is usually applied to older birds. A brace of partridges is *Accolade de perdreaux.*

Peahen—*Paonne.*

Pheasant—*Faisan.*

Pigeons—*Pigeons.*

Young Pigeons—*Pigeonneaux.*
Bardés aux feuilles de vignes they are roasted with vine leaves and slices of bacon over the breasts.

Pintail—*Pilet.*

Plovers—*Pluviers.*

Fat Pullet—*Poularde.*

Quails—*Cailles.* They are *bardées aux feuilles de vignes* in the same way as Pigeons.

Rabbit—*Lapin.*

Young Rabbit—*Lapereau.* A brace of young rabbits—*Accolade de lapereaux.*

Shovellers—*Rouges de rivière.*

Roasts.

Snipes—*Bécassines.*

Teal—*Sarcelle.* They are served *au cresson* with watercress; and *à la Bigarade* with Bigarade sauce.

Turkey—*Dindon* (m.), or *Dinde* (f.).

Turkey Poult—*Dindonneau.* They are *piqué*, larded; *bardé*, barded; and *farci*, stuffed with forcemeat and truffles.

Widgeon—*Canard siffleur.* They are sometimes called *Macreuses.*

Wild Duck—*Canard*, or *Caneton, sauvage.*

Woodcocks—*Bécasses.* Served *à la Piémontaise* they have game sauce and slices of truffles.

CHAPTER VI.

VEGETABLES, OR LÉGUMES, AND SALADS.

ARTICHOKES.

ARTICHOKES plainly boiled are served with butter sauce in a sauce boat as *Artichauts sauce au beurre*, or with Dutch sauce, *sauce Hollandaise*. Artichoke bottoms as:

Artichauts *à la bonne femme* are boiled and served with white sauce.
— *à la Bruxellaise* are cut in quarters, cooked in white sauce, and arranged in a border with Brussels sprouts and Maître d'hôtel sauce in the centre.
— *au velouté* are dressed in the same way and served in the sauce with cream and yolks of eggs.
— *à la Lyonnaise*—cooked in butter and served in brown sauce with onions, &c.
— *à l'Italienne*—cooked in stock, wine, &c., and served in Italian sauce.
— *farcis*—stuffed, and cooked with oil and bacon, &c.
— *à l'essence de jambon*—stuffed, braised, and served covered with a purée of ham.

Artichauts *à la barigoule* — stuffed with chopped bacon, mushrooms, &c.; braised and served with Italian sauce.

—— *farcis à l'Italienne*—the stuffing is made of onion, breadcrumbs and grated cheese.

—— *à la Hollandaise*—stuffed with a purée made from the leaves, and served with Hollandaise sauce.

—— *en mayonnaise*—served cold, coated with Mayonnaise sauce and sprinkled with chopped parsley.

Crème d'artichauts is a purée of artichokes with cream, steamed in a mould; served with cream sauce.

JERUSALEM ARTICHOKES.

Topinambours *à l'Italienne* are cut in fancy shapes, cooked with butter, stock, &c., and glazed; served with Italian sauce. They are also *sauté* in thin slices.

A purée of Jerusalem artichokes with cream, sprinkled with grated Parmesan and browned, is called *Topinambours au gratin*.

ASPARAGUS.

Plainly boiled they are called *Asperges en branches*.

They are served *à la sauce*, with white sauce; *au beurre*, with butter sauce; *à l'huile*, with oil and vinegar.

Asperges *à la crème* are cut up and served in Béchamel sauce.

—— *à la Pompadour*—cut up and served in a sauce of butter, yolks of eggs, &c.

Cut up small, they are dressed *en petits pois*—stewed and served in a white sauce; as *Pointes d'asperges au jus*—stewed in stock; or *à la crème*—served in a sauce of butter, cream, yolks of eggs, &c.

FRENCH BEANS.

Cut in strips and boiled, they are served as:

Haricots verts *à l'Anglaise* on a piece of butter, with chopped parsley.

—— *à la maître d'hôtel*—with Maître d'hôtel sauce.

—— *au beurre noir*—with black-butter sauce.

—— *aux fines herbes*—with a sauce of butter, chopped parsley and shallots, &c.

—— *à la Poulette*—in a white sauce with chopped parsley, &c.

—— *sautés* are sauté in butter with chopped parsley, &c.

Haricots panachés à la Maître d'hôtel are French beans and haricot beans with Maître d'hôtel sauce.

HARICOT BEANS.

White haricot beans, boiled, are served as:

Haricots blancs *à la Maître d'hôtel*, or *à la Bretonne*—with Maître d'hôtel or Bretonne sauce; *au beurre de piment*—with capsicums pounded with butter; *à la moelle*—with beef marrow, &c.

—— *au jus* are stewed in stock.

They are also served *en purée* with stock; or as *Purée de haricots à la crème*—a purée with cream.

Haricots rouges à la Bourguignonne are red haricot beans cooked in stock with onions, wine, &c.

BROAD BEANS.

Fèves de marais *à l'Anglaise* are boiled and served with parsley and butter.

—— *à la crème* are boiled in milk with chopped parsley; served in the sauce with cream, &c.

Purée de fèves is a purée of beans.

BEETROOT.

Cut in slices, beetroot is served as:

Betteraves *à la crème*, boiled in white sauce.

—— *à la Poitevine*—served in brown sauce with onion, spice, &c.

—— *à la Chartreuse*—sandwiches of a slice of

onion between slices of yellow beetroot, dipped in batter and fried.

Broccoli is dressed in the same way as cauliflower.

BRUSSELS SPROUTS.

Choux de Bruxelles *à la Maître d'hotel* are boiled, and served in Maître d'hôtel sauce. *Sautés*, they are sauté in butter with lemon, &c.

CABBAGE.

Choux *farcis*—the heart is cut out, and a stuffing of sausage-meat, &c., put between each leaf. It is braised and served in the sauce.

——— *en surprise*—the heart cut out, it is filled with sausage-meat and boiled chestnuts, and stewed.

CARDOONS.

Boiled cardoons are served *au velouté* in white sauce; *à l'Espagnole* in brown sauce; or *au gratin* covered with breadcrumbs, sprinkled with melted butter, and browned. If grated cheese is mixed with the breadcrumbs, they are called *à l'Italienne*.

Cardons *au jus* are stewed, and served in brown sauce with beef marrow. Garnished with pieces of toast spread with beef marrow, they are called *à la Moelle*.

A purée of cardoons with cream, &c., garnished with croûtons, is served as *Purée de cardons aux croûtons.*

CARROTS.

Boiled and cut in shapes, carrots are served as:

Carottes *à la Béchamel,* in Béchamel sauce, garnished with croûtons; or *à la poulette,* glazed, and served in Poulette sauce.
—— *à la ménagère* are cut in slices and served in a white sauce with wine, herbs, &c.
—— *aux petits pois*—cut in dice and served with peas in a white sauce.
—— *au sucre*—mashed, and dressed with milk, sugar, eggs, &c., the top sprinkled with sugar.

Young carrots stewed in white sauce are called *Petites carottes,* or *Carottes nouvelles, à la sauce blanche.*

Stewed and glazed, they are *glacées;* or *à l'allemande,* served with Allemande or brown sauce.

CAULIFLOWERS.

Chouxfleurs *au gratin* are masked with a white sauce with grated Parmesan, breadcrumbed and browned. They may also be called *au Parmesan.*
—— *sauce au beurre* are served with butter sauce.

Chouxfleurs *à la sauce*—served with white sauce.

Pieces of cauliflower, masked with white sauce, dipped in batter and fried, are called *Marinade de chouxfleurs*.

CELERY.

Céleri *au jus* is stewed in stock.
—— *à la moelle* is stewed and served on toast, with brown sauce and beef marrow.
—— *à la crème*—stewed, and served in a white sauce with cream.
—— *à l'Espagnole*—stewed, and served in Espagnole sauce.
—— *à la Chetwynd*—stewed with onions, and served on toast with the onions, and Béchamel sauce with cream, &c.
—— *à la Villeroi*—masked with Allemande sauce, breadcrumbed and fried.

Celery roots are served with butter sauce as *Celeri-rave à la sauce au beurre*; stewed and served *au jus*; or glazed—*à la demi glace*. They are also dressed as a *Purée de céleri-rave*.

CHESTNUTS.

Though properly a fruit, a purée of chestnuts cooked with stock and wine may be served as a vegetable, and called *Purée de marrons*.

CUCUMBER.

Slices of cucumber cooked with cream, butter and flour are called *Concombres à la crème*.

Concombres *à la poulette*—cut in pieces, and cooked with butter and sugar; served in white sauce with cream, chopped parsley, &c.

—— *farcies à la crème*—the centres scooped out, they are stuffed and stewed; served in Béchamel sauce with cream and sugar.

—— *à l'Espagnole*—cut in short lengths, stuffed, stewed, and served with brown sauce.

—— *à la moëlle*—the stuffing is made of bread-crumbs, beef marrow, &c.; they are served with a brown sauce.

EGG PLANT.

Aubergines *farcies* are cut in halves, the centres chopped, and put back into the skins with oil, brown sauce, &c.; sprinkled with breadcrumbs and browned.

ENDIVE.

Chicorée *au jus* is stewed in stock.

—— *à la crème* is chopped, and dressed with cream, white sauce, &c.; garnished with croûtons. If the cream is omitted, it should be called *en purée*.

LEEKS.

As *Poireaux au jus* they are stewed in stock.

LENTILS.

A purée of lentils with stock, garnished with croûtons, is served as *Purée de lentilles aux croûtons*.

LETTUCE.

Lettuce is served *au jus*, stewed; or as *Laitues farcies*, the centres cut out, filled with forcemeat and braised.

MORELS.

Morilles *aux croûtons* are stewed and served with the sauce on buttered toast.

—— *à l'Italienne* are served in Italian sauce.

—— *à l'Andalouse* are cooked with oil, wine, ham, &c., and served in the sauce.

MUSHROOMS.

For *Croûtes aux champignons* they are broiled and served on toast.

Champignons *à la sauce* are stewed, and served in white sauce.

—— *à la Bordelaise* are soaked in oil, broiled, and served in the oil with chopped parsley, &c.

—— *farcis* or *au gratin* are filled with stuffing, sprinkled with breadcrumbs and baked. They are served with or without brown sauce.

Cut in slices they are dressed *en ragoût*, with broth, chopped parsley, &c ; or *à la crème*, with butter, cream, &c.

For *Purée de champignons* they are chopped, and served with butter, gravy, &c., garnished with croûtons.

ONIONS.

Stewed Portugal onions are served as *Oignons au jus*.

Stewed in a white sauce with purée of ham they are *en ragoût*.

For *Oignons farcis* the centres are cut out, they are stuffed, and cooked with bacon, &c.

Small onions served in Poulette sauce are *à la poulette*.

Au sirop doré they are stewed with butter, sugar, &c., and are served in the sauce.

A purée of onions with stock is called *Purée*

d'oignons à la Bretonne. It is garnished with croûtons.

PEAS.

Petits pois *à l'Anglaise* are boiled and served on a lump of butter.

—— *à la Française* are stewed, and mixed with flour and butter.

—— *à la Parisienne*—boiled with onions, butter, sugar, &c., and served with the sauce.

—— *au jus*—stewed in stock.

—— *aux laitues*—stewed with lettuces.

—— *à l'ancienne mode*—stewed, and served with cream and yolk of egg.

They are also served *au lard*, stewed in stock with dice of bacon, &c.; or *au jambon* with dice of ham, young onions, &c.

—— *en cosses* are boiled in their shells.

POTATOES.

Pommes de terre *en chemise* are boiled in their skins.

Boiled and cut in slices they are served *à l'anglaise*, with butter; *à la maître d'hôtel*, in maître d'hôtel sauce; or *à la crème au gratin*, with white sauce and grated Parmesan, sprinkled with breadcrumbs and browned.

Pommes de terre *à la Parisienne* are cooked in butter and water with onions, &c.

—— *au lard*—cut in slices and cooked in a white sauce with dice of bacon, &c.

—— *à la crème*—cut in slices, and served in white sauce.

—— *sautées*—cut in slices and fried.

—— *à la Macaire*—fried potato trimmings.

—— *à la Lyonnaise*—cut in slices and sauté in butter with shallot, &c. If oil is used instead of butter they are called *à la Provençale*.

—— *soufflées*—baked in their skins; the potatoes mixed with butter, grated Parmesan, eggs, &c., put back into the skins and browned.

—— *à l'Italienne* are dressed in the same way, but the potato pulp is mixed with rice, grated Parmesan, &c.

—— *nouvelles à la crème* are young potatoes boiled in cream with chopped parsley, &c.

Croquettes de pommes de terre are potato croquettes, breadcrumbed and fried. This paste sauté in small shapes, and dressed in a crown with white sauce, is called *Pommes de terre à la Duchesse*. It is also made into *quenelles*.

Croquettes de pommes de terre à la Béchamel are potato croquettes with Béchamel sauce.

A purée of potatoes as *Purée de pommes de terre*

gratinée is sprinkled with breadcrumbs and browned. Mixed with white sauce it is called *à la Maria*.

PURSLANE.

The stalks of Purslane with cinnamon, &c., dipped in batter and fried, are called *Pourpier en friture à la Milanaise*.

SALSIFIS.

Salsifis *à la crème* is boiled and served in a white sauce.
—— *à la Béchamel* is served in Béchamel sauce.
—— *à la moëlle*—stewed, and served with beef marrow spread on pieces of toast, and brown sauce.
—— *à la poulette*—served in white sauce with cream, mushrooms, &c.
—— *frits*—soaked in oil, &c., breadcrumbed and fried. If the pieces are dipped in batter and fried they are called *Beignets de salsifis*.

SEA-KALE.

Boiled sea-kale served on toast with butter sauce is called *Choux de mer à la sauce* ; *à l'Espagnole*, it is served in Espagnole sauce.

SPINACH.

Spinach is served *à l'Anglaise*, with butter or cream; *à la Française* with butter, stock, &c.

Épinards *à l'Allemande*—dressed with butter, cream, breadcrumbs, &c.

—— *au velouté*—with velouté sauce.

—— *à la crème*—with cream and sugar.

—— *au jus* is stewed, and served with gravy.

—— *au sucre*—cooked in butter and mixed with sugar, &c.

TOMATOES.

Tomates *farcies* or *au gratin*—the centres are cut out, they are stuffed, sprinkled with breadcrumbs and baked.

—— *à la Provençale*—the centres are mixed with oil, chopped onions, &c, put back into the skins and baked.

Soufflé de tomates is tomato pulp with eggs, baked in small soufflé cases.

TRUFFLES.

Truffes *à la serviette* are cooked in wine and broth, and served on a napkin.

Truffes *sous la cendre*—wrapped in slices of bacon and paper, and broiled in hot cinders.

—— *au vin de champagne*—cooked with bacon, veal, mushrooms, champagne, &c.; and served in the sauce.

—— *à la Piémontaise*—cut in slices, fried in oil with garlic, &c., and served with Italian sauce on buttered crusts of rolls.

—— *demi Piémontaise* are dressed in the same way, substituting tomato sauce with wine and garlic for Italian sauce.

—— *à la Dino*—truffles dressed "au vin de champagne" are used for this dish. The centres chopped with forcemeat, &c., put back into the shells, braised, and served with truffle sauce.

For *Croûtes aux truffes* they are cut in slices, cooked in brown sauce with wine, &c., and served on toast.

TURNIPS.

Navets *au jus* are stewed in stock and served in the sauce.

—— *au sucre* are stewed with stock and sugar.

—— *glacés au jus*—stewed and glazed in stock.

—— *glacés au sucre*—cooked with butter, sugar and stock, and glazed.

—— *à la Poulette*—cut in shapes and cooked in white sauce.

They are also served in a purée, garnished with croûtons, as *Purée de navets.*

VEGETABLE MARROW.

Potirons, or **Giraumons,** *à la Hollandaise* are cut in pieces, baked, and served in Hollandaise sauce.

—— *à la Provençale* are cut in halves, fried, and filled with a stuffing of onions, breadcrumbs, oil, &c.

—— *au gratin*—a purée of vegetable marrow with cream, sprinkled with breadcrumbs and browned.

YAMS or SWEET POTATOES.

Patates *au beurre* are cooked, cut in slices and served with butter.

—— *à la Française* are cut in pieces, and served in a sauce of butter, flour, cream, &c.

For *Beignets de patates* they are cut in pieces, soaked in brandy, dipped in batter and fried.

Chartreuse *de légumes* is an ornamental mould of mixed vegetables, filled with chopped vegetables stewed in brown sauce.

K

Racines *en menu droits* are slices of onions, carrots and turnips, &c., with mustard and vinegar.

SALADS.

Salade *à la Macédoine de légumes* is composed of separate heaps of vegetables, with oil and vinegar.

—— *de pommes de terre*—slices of potatoes and beetroot, with chopped parsley, &c., oil and vinegar.

—— *de cresson aux pommes de terre*—watercress and slices of potatoes, with oil and vinegar.

—— *de tomates*—slices of raw tomatoes with chopped shallots, &c., oil and vinegar.

—— *de choux rouges à la Russe*—red cabbage, with sauce of sour cream, hard-boiled yolks of eggs, &c.

—— *aux concombres*—slices of cucumber with oil and vinegar.

—— *aux betteraves*—slices of beetroot, with chopped Portugal onions, oil and vinegar.

—— *de chicorée à la Française*—endive, with oil, vinegar and garlic.

—— *à la Française*—lettuce, or any one kind of salad only, with oil, vinegar, &c.

—— *à l'Anglaise*—lettuce, celery, beetroot, endive, &c., with oil and vinegar.

—— *à l'Allemande*—slices of potatoes, Brussels

sprouts, cauliflower and celery, with oil, vinegar, &c.

Salade *à l'Italienne*—several kinds of salad and vegetables, with meat or fish, anchovies, olives, &c., and Tartare sauce.

—— *à la Flamande*—Dutch herrings, or any dried fish, pickled shrimps, apples, beetroot, potatoes, &c., with oil and vinegar.

—— *à l'Espagnole*—a border of slices of tomatoes, and pickled onions with Mayonnaise sauce in the centre.

—— *à la Russe*—carrots, parsnips and beetroot cut in shapes, pieces of fowl or game, anchovies, olives, Russian caviare, &c., with oil, vinegar and mustard.

Another way of serving it is a mould of vegetables with yolks of eggs, cream, purée of spinach, &c.

—— *à la Cazanova*—dice of ham and fish, with celery, hard-boiled whites of eggs, &c. Mayonnaise sauce with powdered yolks of eggs.

—— *à la Tartare*—lettuce, with pickled cucumbers, onions, &c., herrings cut in dice, oil and vinegar.

—— *à la Demidoff*—slices of potatoes and truffles, with oil and vinegar, young onions, &c.

—— *à Madame*—lettuce, with sauce of oil, vinegar, yolk of egg, &c.

Salade *à la Jardinière*—fine strips of vegetables, with oil, vinegar, &c.

Cerises *à la vinaigrette* is composed of stoned cherries, fillets of anchovies, young onions, chopped bacon, &c., with oil, vinegar, mustard and spice.

CHAPTER VII.

EGGS AND OMELETTES.

EGGS.

POACHED eggs, or *Œufs pochés*, may be served *au jus*, with brown gravy, garnished with fillets of anchovy placed crosswise on each egg; or *au jambon*, on oval slices of fried ham, with Poivrade sauce.

So-called "buttered" eggs—cooked with butter, &c.—are served as *Œufs brouillés*.

- Œufs *brouillés aux pointes d'asperges, aux champignons, aux truffes*, or *au jambon*, are dressed in the same way, with the addition of asparagus cut up, chopped mushrooms, truffles, or ham.
- —— *brouillés à l'Indienne* are cooked with butter, chopped onion, curry powder, &c.
- —— *au beurre noir*—fried, and served in black-butter sauce.
- —— *à la Suisse* are baked in a dish lined with slices of cheese, covered with cream and sprinkled with grated cheese.

Œufs *au kari,* or *à l'Indienne,* are poached in a sauce of milk, butter, onions, curry powder, &c.

—— *au miroir* are baked with butter, &c., in the dish in which they are served.

—— *aux pistaches*—mixed with cream, pounded pistachio nuts, &c., and baked.

—— *à la bonne femme*—baked with chopped onions and vinegar.

—— *au soleil*—poached, dipped in a batter and fried.

—— *à la neige*—spoonfuls of whipped whites poached in milk, &c.; served in the milk with yolks of eggs.

—— *en caisse*—cooked in little soufflé cases half filled with breadcrumbs.

—— *au bouillon*—steamed with stock in little moulds; served with gravy.

—— *à la Provençale*—cooked in small moulds with brown sauce, chopped onions, &c., and served with brown sauce.

—— *à la Béchamel* are hard-boiled, cut in halves, and served in Béchamel sauce.

—— *au velouté*—hard-boiled, cut in slices and served in white sauce.

—— *à la Tripe*—slices of eggs with slices of onions, and Béchamel sauce with garlic, &c.

—— *au gratin*—slices in layers with white sauce, grated Parmesan, &c.; sprinkled with breadcrumbs and grated Parmesan, and baked.

Œufs *à l'aurore*—shred hard-boiled whites of eggs in Aurora sauce, in layers with grated Parmesan and the yolks of the eggs powdered.

—— *à la St. James*—boiled hard in moulds, the yolks mixed with chopped truffles and put back into the whites; served in Mayonnaise sauce with chopped truffles.

—— *en canapés*—hard-boiled and cut in halves, the yolks mixed with chopped parsley, butter, &c, and put back into the whites.

—— *farcis à la crème* are prepared in the same way, and served with Béchamel sauce.

—— *en aspic*—slices of hard-boiled eggs set in a mould of aspic.

Plovers' or Lapwings' eggs are set in a mould of aspic, or served with a border of aspic round them, as *Œufs de pluviers*, or *vanneaux*, *en aspic*, or *à l'aspic*.

OMELETTES.

A simple omelette is called *Omelette au naturel*.

Omelette *aux fines herbes* is a savoury omelette —with chopped parsley and shallot.

—— *au Parmesan*—with grated Parmesan; if Gruyère cheese is used instead of Parmesan it is called *au fromage*.

Omelette *au jambon*—with chopped ham.

—— *au lard*—with chopped fried bacon.

—— *à la purée de volaille,* or *gibier,* has some of the purée in the centre of the omelette.

—— *aux truffes* has slices of truffles in brown sauce in the centre of the omelette.

—— *aux champignons*—with mushrooms in brown sauce in the centre.

—— *aux tomates*—with dressed tomatoes in the centre of the omelette.

—— *aux olives*—with olives and brown sauce in the centre.

—— *aux huîtres*—with oysters in white sauce in the centre.

—— *aux rognons*—kidneys with fine herbs in the centre of a savoury omelette.

—— *aux anchois* has fillets of anchovy on pieces of toast in the centre; it is served with gravy.

—— *à la Jardinière* is made with chopped vegetables mixed with the eggs.

In addition to these there are the sweet omelettes—*au sucre.*

Omelette *aux confitures*—a sweet omelette folded over jam.

—— *au rhum*—a sweet omelette with rum, and a sauce of burning rum.

—— *à la Celestine*—a small omelette of sugar,

flour, milk and eggs, with apricot marmalade and frangipane in the centre.

An *Omelette soufflée* is made with sugar, beaten yolks and beaten whites of eggs, and is baked.

For *Omelette soufflée à la crème*, whipped cream is used instead of some of the whites of eggs.

CHAPTER VIII.

ENTREMETS.

CAKES AND PASTRY.

Gâteau *Napolitaine* is a cake composed of thin round pieces of a paste of pounded almonds, flour, butter, yolks of eggs, &c., spread with preserve and piled one on the other. Garnished with pistachio nuts, or masked with the preserve, or glazed with sugar icing. It is sometimes called *Gâteau Napolitaine à la Chantilly.*

—— *à la Compiègne* is a cake of flour, butter, eggs, cream, &c.; cut in slices, spread with apricot marmalade, and put together again.

—— *à la Victoria*—a cake of flour, butter, eggs, dried cherries, citron, cream, &c.; served with almond custard.

—— *d'amandes*—a cake of ground almonds, eggs, sugar, &c.

—— *de pistaches* is made in the same way with pistachio nuts instead of almonds.

Gâteau *Saint Louis*—a cake of flour, butter, whites of eggs, almonds, &c., in a shell of paste; sprinkled with chopped almonds.

—— *Saint Charles* is an almond cake baked in a mould lined with paste.

—— *de riz*—rice cake. Served *au caramel* it has burnt sugar sauce.

—— *de riz à la bourgeoise*—a rice cake baked in a mould lined with breadcrumbs; served with any fruit sauce.

—— *de semoule*—semolina cake. Served with cream it is called *à la crème*.

Baba *au rhum*—a cake of flour, butter, eggs, sultana raisins, citron, &c., baked in a mould decreasing in stages, and served with a sauce of apricot syrup and rum. It is sometimes called *Baba à la Polonaise*.

Brioche *à la crème*—a cake of flour, butter, eggs, whipped cream, &c. If served with stewed fruit it is called *Brioche aux fruits*.

Gâteau *de mille feuilles*—a pile of thin round pieces of puff paste, spread alternately with apricot marmalade, orange marmalade and currant jelly. Masked with apricot marmalade, and garnished with dried cherries.

—— *Génoise*—little shapes or cakes made of a batter of pounded almonds, sugar, flour, eggs, whipped cream, &c., decorated with pink and white icing. The small shapes are sometimes called *Génoises glacés à l'Italienne.*

There are various other ways in which this is served. As *Gâteau génoise aux abricots* it is a cake cut in slices, spread with apricot marmalade, and put together again; covered with the marmalade, and served with whipped cream.

Génoises aux amandes are masked with meringue mixture, and sprinkled with chopped almonds, &c.

Pâtisserie génoise is Genoese pastry made of flour, butter, sugar, eggs and brandy, cut into sandwiches with jam.

A Genoese cake is served in this way as *Biscuits à la Vénitienne,* coated with pink and white icing sugar. As *Puits d'amour* it is cut in shapes an inch thick, the centres cut out, and the space filled with whipped cream and preserve. The whole glazed with sugar icing. These are also made with pound cake instead of Genoese.

Biscuit de Savoie is Savoy or sponge cake.

Any cake cut in small shapes and glazed with chocolate is served as *Chocolat glacé.* Sponge biscuits glazed with chocolate are called *Biscuit glacé au chocolat.*

Petits pains *à la Parisienne* are sandwiches of finger biscuits with preserve, masked with alternate lines of meringue mixture and preserve.

Petits gâteaux *aux amandes* are small shapes of a paste of flour, sugar, eggs, almonds, &c., with chopped almonds strewn on the top; they are served with whipped cream or preserve in the centre of the dish.

—— *à l'Irlandaise*—small cakes of a batter of flour, butter, eggs, &c.

Gâteaux *à la reine*—small shapes of a paste of pounded almonds, sugar and whites of eggs; glazed with sugar icing.

Petits gâteaux *à la Victoria*—little cakes of flour, butter, pounded almonds, maraschino, &c., spread with orange marmalade, and glazed with yellow icing.

Madeleines are little cakes of a batter of flour, butter, eggs, brandy, &c.

Darioles—a batter of flour, sugar, eggs, cream, pounded almonds, &c., baked in dariole moulds lined with paste, with candied orange flowers on the top. Flavoured with vanilla or coffee they are called *à la vanille*, or *au café*.

—— *à la Duchesse* are Duchess cakes made of a batter of flour, eggs, citron, angelica, dried cherries, &c.; glazed with white sugar.

—— *à la patissière* are small cakes of sugar, flour, butter, cream, yolks of eggs, &c.

Biscuits *à l'Italienne* are fancy shapes of a paste of flour, sugar, eggs, chopped almonds, &c., spread with jam, and put together in pairs. They are served in a crown with whipped cream in the centre.

—— *aux pêches* are round-topped biscuits spread with jam and put together in pairs in the shape of peaches; coated with white icing and a little red colouring.

—— *aux abricots* are made in the same way, but of a smaller size. Apricot jam should be used, and yellow icing.

Gâteaux *à la crème*—pastry of cream, flour and butter, in fancy shapes.

Gâteau *feuilleté* is puff paste cut in shapes.

Puit de fruits aux blanches couronnes is formed of rings of puff paste spread with preserve, and put one on the other in a pile; garnished with angelica, and a piping of whipped cream; the centre filled with stewed fruit.

Gâteaux *à la Condé*—thin oblong or fancy shapes of puff paste, the surface covered with chopped almonds, sugar, &c. This is sometimes called *Pâtisserie d'amandes à la Condé*.

Petits gâteaux *d'abricots* are square pieces of puff paste folded over apricot marmalade.

—— *à la Polonaise* are little folded envelopes

of puff paste, garnished with red currant jelly.

Éventail aux cerises—strips of puff paste on a border of apple marmalade with stewed cherries in the centre.

Petits vol-au-vents *à la Chantilly* are little vol-au-vents of puff paste filled with marmalade and cream "à la Chantilly."

—— *à la gelée mousseuse* are covered with chopped sugar coloured red, and filled with Maraschino jelly whipped to a froth. As *Petits puits aux pistaches* they are covered with chopped pistachio nuts and sugar, and filled with whipped cream.

Pâtisserie *à la tartine*—sandwiches of puff paste and jam.

Gauffres *à la Française*—a batter of flour, sugar, whipped cream, eggs, &c., baked in gauffre irons.

—— *à l'Allemande, à la Flamande,* and *de Carlsbad,* are varieties of the French gauffres.

—— *aux amandes*—a batter of flour, sugar, almonds, eggs, &c., baked in thin pieces, coiled round and filled with whipped cream.

Suédoises *à la crème*—a batter of flour, sugar, almonds, &c., baked in small balls, and served with whipped cream.

Petits choux are Spanish cakes made of a batter of flour, butter, eggs, sugar, &c., baked in small balls. They are served *aux amandes*, or *à la crème*, covered with chopped almonds and sugar, or filled with cream; *au caramel* they are dipped in boiled sugar and covered with chopped pistachio nuts and sugar.

—— *à l'Espagnole* are fried in the shape of small balls. *À la comtesse* they are baked in finger-shaped pieces and filled with cream; *en gimblettes*, deep rings of the paste are covered with chopped pistachio nuts and sugar.

Petits pains *de la Mecque*, or Mecca loaves, are small oval cakes made of the same paste with the addition of whipped cream; sprinkled with chopped sugar. Flavoured with lemon they are called *Petits pains de la Mecque au citron*.

Soupirs de nonne, or *Pets de nonne*, are made of a paste of butter, sugar, flour, eggs, orange-flower water, &c., fried in small balls. This paste, in the shape of fingers, glazed with chocolate, is called *Éclairs au chocolat*.

Profiterolles—small oval cakes of milk, butter, sugar, eggs, &c.; served with chocolate sauce.

Gâteaux *fourrés aux confitures* are jam turnovers or puffs.

—— *fourrés à la crème* are turnovers or puffs filled with frangipane.

—— *fourrés de pommes à la Parisienne* are paste turnovers filled with stewed apples and apricot marmalade.

—— *d'Artois,* or *à la Manon,* are small covered puff-paste tarts or tartlets filled with any kind of preserve. Filled with apricot jam they may be called *D'Artois aux abricots.*

Mince pies are called *Pâtés d'émincé.*

Tartlets are filled with any kind of preserve, and take their name from it—as *Tartelettes de fraises, aux cerises, aux prunes,* &c. ; *à la vanille* they are filled with pounded almonds, vanilla sugar, whipped whites of eggs, &c.

Tartelettes *de crème à la Frangipane* are filled with frangipane.

—— *à la Mosaïque* are filled with preserve, and covered with a mosaic of paste.

—— *à la Pompadour* are filled with a ball of brioche paste folded over apricot or other marmalade, and sprinkled with sugar.

Dauphines are tartlets filled with preserve, with

custard over it, and Meringue mixture piled on the top.

Fanchonettes are tartlets filled with custard, meringued over, and the tops ornamented with little miniature meringues. In *Fanchonettes à la vanille* the custard is flavoured with vanilla.

Mirlitons *aux fleurs d'oranger* are tartlets filled with a batter of eggs, sugar, butter, pounded macaroons, candied orange flowers, &c. They are flavoured in various ways— *aux amandes*, with almonds instead of the orange flowers; or *au chocolat*, with chocolate. *Aux confitures* they are half filled with jam before the batter is put in.

Talmouses are cheese-cakes.

—— *au citron*—lemon cheese-cakes.

—— *aux amandes* are made of pounded almonds with sugar, butter, ground rice and eggs.

—— *aux oranges*—made of pounded almonds, orange-flower water, sugar, butter and eggs, with orange marmalade.

Of the fruit tarts there are *Tarte aux abricots*— apricots; *aux prunes* -plums; *aux prunes reine-claude*—greengages; *de pêches*—peaches; *de pommes*—apples; *de pommes aux coings*—apple with quince; *de poires*—pears; *de framboises et groseilles*—raspberries and currants; *de groseilles vertes* or *à maquereau*—green gooseberries; *de groseilles*—currants; *de cassis*—black currants; *de raisins verts*—green grapes; *de cerises*—cherries; *de rhubarbe*—rhubarb.

Tourte *à la crème d'amandes* is an open tart filled with almond cream.

—— *à la frangipane* is an open tart filled with Frangipane—a custard of flour, eggs, cream, butter or beef marrow, &c.

—— *d'abricots à l'Allemande*—an open tart filled with apricots, and apricot marmalade over them.

Flan *de poires, de cerises, de fraises,* &c., are open fruit tarts.

—— *d'oranges* is an open tart filled with stewed oranges.

—— *d'amandes à la d'Escars*—an open tart filled with a custard of green almonds with candied orange flowers, yolks of eggs, cream, &c. This is also made with filberts.

—— *à la crème pralinée* is filled with custard, and is sprinkled with sugar and glazed.

—— *d'abricots à la Metternich* is filled with apricots and cherries, and the pounded kernels with cream on the top.

Pommes en croustade is a baked shape of paste filled with stewed apples, and garnished with dried cherries.

Apple dumplings are called *Dumplings aux pommes*.

PUDDINGS.

Plum pouding—Plum pudding.
Pouding *au riz*—Rice pudding.
―― *au tapioca*—Tapioca pudding.
―― *au sagou*—Sago pudding.
―― *à la semoule*—Semolina pudding.
―― *au macaroni*—Macaroni pudding.
―― *au vermicelle*—Vermicelli pudding.
―― *à la crème de riz*—Ground rice pudding.
―― *au pain*—Bread-and-butter pudding. Another pudding "au pain" is made of breadcrumbs, milk, eggs, lemon peel, &c.
―― *au pain bis*—Brown-bread pudding.
―― *aux abricots*—breadcrumbs, cream, sugar, yolks of eggs and apricots, baked in a mould lined with paste.
―― *aux groseilles*—a purée of gooseberries, with breadcrumbs, eggs, &c.; baked in a mould lined with paste.
―― *aux marrons*—a mould of chestnut flour, butter, milk, eggs, &c. It is served with apricot syrup or jam.
―― *aux pommes*—a baked pudding of alternate layers of breadcrumbs and apple sauce.

Pouding *aux figues*—a boiled mould of pounded figs, suet, milk, eggs, breadcrumbs, &c.

—— *à l'ananas* — Pine-apple pudding. Whip sauce, with the pineapple syrup, is served with it.

—— *au gingembre*—Ginger pudding.

—— *au citron*—Lemon pudding.

—— *aux oranges* is made in the same way as lemon pudding, with oranges instead of lemons.

—— *au chocolat*—a steamed mould of sponge cake in crumbs, butter, sugar, eggs, chocolate, &c.

—— *au caramel*—custard pudding in a mould with burnt sugar. It is usually served cold, with burnt-sugar sauce, or with burnt brandy and sugar.

—— *à la marmelade*—a steamed mould of flour, brown sugar, milk, eggs, marmalade, &c; served with marmalade sauce.

—— *soufflé*—a very light steamed pudding; it is served with wine or marmalade sauce, or with a syrup of fruit.

—— *de cabinet,* or *Cabinet pouding*—Cabinet pudding. This is also iced and served as *Pouding de cabinet glacé.*

—— *au biscuit de Savoie*—a sponge cake with brandy, steamed in a mould with custard and dried cherries.

Pouding à la *Snowdon*—a steamed pudding of suet, breadcrumbs, brown sugar and marmalade
—— à la *Cowley*—a pudding of mashed potatoes, almonds, sugar, eggs, &c.; it is served covered with whip sauce.
—— à la *Mousseline*—a steamed pudding of lemon, sugar, butter, eggs, &c.; served with a sweet sauce.
—— à la *Victoria*—a pudding of flour, breadcrumbs, dried cherries, candied peel, cream, eggs, brandy, &c.; served with whip sauce.
—— à l'*Allemande*—a mould of bread cut in dice, almonds, raisins, sugar, custard, wine, &c.; served with whip sauce.
—— *Génoise*—Genoese pastry spread with preserve and rolled.
—— *Nesselrode*, or à la *Nesselrode*—Ice pudding.
Croquettes de *riz* are rice croquettes.
—— de *crème de riz*—Ground-rice croquettes.
—— de *semoule*—Semolina croquettes.
—— de *vermicelle*—Vermicelli croquettes.
Croustade de riz is a fancy mould of rice, the centre filled with a cornflour custard.
Riz meringue—rice, with milk, cream, sugar, whites of eggs, &c.; sprinkled with sugar and baked.
Dumpling ferme—small balls of a paste of flour,

water and currants; served with wine sauce.

Quenelles à la crème are small quenelles of a paste of flour, cream, eggs, &c. They are also made *à la semoule* with semolina.

Soupe dorée, or *Pain perdu*—small shapes of bread, soaked in milk, &c., dipped in beaten eggs and fried.

FRITTERS.

Beignets *d'abricots à la Chartres* are apricot fritters.

—— *d'abricots à l'eau de vie*—sandwiches of bread dipped in brandy, and half apricots; fried in batter.

—— *de pêches à la royale*—peach fritters.

—— *de pêches au vin du Rhin*—half peaches soaked in Rhine wine, &c., and fried; served in a syrup of the wine with the kernels.

—— *de pommes à la d'Orléans*—apple fritters.

—— *de pommes à la Bavarie*—apples soaked in brandy, &c., floured and fried.

—— *de poires*—pear fritters.

—— *de fraises à la Dauphine*—strawberry fritters.

—— *de groseilles à la Dauphine*—currant fritters.

—— *d'ananas*—pine-apple fritters.

Beignets *d'oranges*—orange fritters.
—— *de fleurs de sureau*—fritters of sprigs of elder flowers
—— *à la crème* are custard fritters.
—— *aux confitures*—small sandwiches of cake and jam, dipped in batter with wine, and fried.
—— *au riz*—round or oval pieces of a paste of ground rice with milk, eggs, &c., breadcrumbed and fried.
—— *à la bonne femme*—small fried balls of a paste of butter, sugar, eggs, &c.
—— *à la Chantilly* are made of a batter of flour, eggs, cream cheese, wine, &c.
—— *de Cintra*—thin round slices of cake soaked in cream, &c., floured and fried.
—— *à l'Allemande*—small round sandwiches of brioche paste and preserve; fried.
—— *à la Prussienne* are the same made of puff paste, with apple marmalade.
—— *à l'Espagnole*—small pieces of crumb of French roll soaked in cream, &c., and fried.
—— *à la Portugaise*—balls of a paste of rice, milk, sugar, eggs, &c, with marmalade in the centre; breadcrumbed and fried.
—— *en surprise*—apples with the stalks left on, soaked in brandy, &c., filled with apricot jam, dipped in batter and fried.

Beignets soufflés *à la vanille* are small fried balls of a batter flavoured with vanilla.
—— *aux fleurs d'oranger* are flavoured with orange-flower water.
—— *aux confitures* are served with preserve.
—— *au maizena* are made with maizena.

Crêpes are pancakes.
—— *aux confitures* are spread with preserve and rolled.
—— *au riz* are made of rice with sugar, cream, eggs, &c.
—— *au maizena* are made with maizena.
—— *à la Française*—a batter of eggs, sugar, cream and flour, fried and folded over preserve.

COMPOTES, &c., OF FRUIT.

Compote *d'abricots*—apricots boiled in syrup. It is also made of green apricots.
—— *d'abricots à la Breteuil*—half apricots sprinkled with sugar and broiled; served with apricot and raspberry syrup.

Abricots *au riz* are stewed apricots with rice. Served round a shape of rice, with apricot syrup, they are called *à la Condé*.

Pain d'abricots is a mould of apricot cheese; it is served with cream in the centre.

Meringue *d'abricots*—apricot marmalade with custard over it, and Meringue mixture on the top.

Croûtes aux abricots are fried slices of bread spread with preserved apricots, and served with a syrup of apricots.

Compote *de pêches*—peaches boiled in syrup. They are also dressed *à la Condé*, and as *Pain de pêches* in the same way as apricots.

Chartreuse *de pêches* is a mould ornamentally lined with pieces of peaches, and filled with peach marmalade.

Gâteau *de Mirabelles* is a mould of Mirabelle plum marmalade. Plums are also dressed as *Meringue de prunes* in the same way as apricots.

—— *de prunes à la crème* is a mould of stewed prunes, currant jelly, &c.; served with whipped cream in the centre.

Prunes *au riz* are stewed prunes with rice.

Pain de prunes de damas is a mould of damson cheese or marmalade.

Compote *de prunes reine-claude*—greengages boiled in syrup.

Croûtes aux reine-claude are little patties of fried bread filled with compote of greengages, and the syrup poured round.

Pommes *au beurre* are apples filled with butter and sugar, and baked.

Compotes, &c., of Fruit.

Pommes *au riz* are stewed apples with rice.

—— *au riz en timbale*—a shell of paste filled with rice, and stewed apples in the centre; covered with apricot marmalade.

—— *au riz meringué* are stewed, and served in a border of rice with custard over them, and the whole covered with Meringue mixture.

—— *meringuées* are dressed in the same way without the rice.

—— *à la Condé* are dressed the same as apricots.

—— *à la Portugaise* are baked, and covered with apricot marmalade.

Miroton *de pommes*—stewed apples with melted currant jelly and wine; garnished with dried cherries.

Gâteau *de pommes* is a mould of apple marmalade; served with a custard sauce.

—— *de pommes aux abricots*—a mould of apple marmalade, covered with apricot marmalade.

Pain de pommes à la Russe is a mould of apple marmalade with whipped cream in the centre, and melted currant jelly round.

Croquettes *de pommes* are pieces of apple marmalade, breadcrumbed and fried.

Meringue *de pommes à la Portugaise*—a round shell of paste filled with apple marmalade, with half apples on the top, and a well of custard in the centre; spread with orange marmalade, and covered with Meringue mixture.

Chartreuse *de pommes* is a mould ornamentally lined with slices of apples, coloured pink and yellow, and filled with apple marmalade.

Charlotte *de pommes* is Apple Charlotte. If apricot jam is mixed with the apple marmalade it is called *Charlotte de pommes aux abricots*.

Pears are dressed *au riz*, as *Charlotte de poires*, and in many of the ways given for apples.

Timbale *de poires* is stewed pears in a shell of paste, covered with apricot marmalade.

Compote *de poires au riz*—a compote of pears stewed in syrup, served cold with a border of rice.

—— *de fruits à la Normande* is a mould of pears stewed in cider. Slices of fried bread spread with this compote are called *Croûtes à la Normande*. They are dressed in a circle, with a syrup of the jam with wine in the centre.

Croûtes aux fraises à la Bellerive — strawberries spread on buttered buns.

Pain de framboises et groseilles is a mould of raspberry and currant cheese; it is served with cream in the centre. Black currants are dressed in this way as *Pain de cassis à la crème.*

Compote *d'oranges*—oranges boiled in syrup.

Pain d'ananas is a mould of pine-apple cheese.

Croûtes aux ananas are little patties of fried bread, filled with compote of pine-apples and served with the syrup.

Compote *de marrons*—boiled chestnuts with syrup.

Gâteau *de marrons* is a steamed mould of pounded chestnuts with cream, eggs, &c. Balls of this preparation, breadcrumbed and fried, are served as *Croquettes de marrons.*

Marrons *à la crème* are powdered chestnuts covered with whipped cream.

Châtaignes *croquantes* are small crystallized pieces of pounded chestnuts with sugar, eggs, &c.

Chartreuse *de fruits* is an ornamental mould of fruit.

Macédoine *de fruits* is composed of mixed fruits in syrup. *Au citron* it is flavoured with lemon.

—— *de fruits en gelée* is a mould of alternate layers of the different fruits, and of jelly.

Croûtes aux fruits are fried slices of bread spread

with preserved fruit, and served with a syrup of the fruit.

Petits nougats *à la Chantilly* are small shapes of nougat filled with Chantilly cream.

Croquantes are small pieces of nougat.

CREAMS.

Crème *au chocolat* is chocolate cream. These creams served in little cups, are called *Petits pots de crème au chocolat,* &c.

—— *au café* is coffee cream.

—— *de thé* is tea cream.

—— *de thé vert* is green tea cream.

—— *à la vanille* is vanilla cream.

—— *au ponche* is flavoured with punch.

—— *au noyau* is flavoured with noyau.

—— *au marasquin* is flavoured with maraschino.

—— *aux abricots* is apricot cream.

—— *de fraises* is strawberry cream.

—— *de framboises* is raspberry cream.

—— *à l'ananas* is pineapple cream.

—— *aux mille fruits* is made with preserved strawberries, raspberries, apricots, plums and other fruits.

—— *d'oranges* is orange cream.

—— *d'amandes* is almond cream.

—— *aux fleurs d'oranger* is made of fresh orange flowers boiled in cream.

Creams.

Crème *brulée,* or *au caramel,* is made of yolks of eggs, milk, burnt sugar, &c.

—— *de velours* is made of cream, sugar, wine, &c.

—— *au gelée*—a mould of whipped jelly and cream.

—— *vierge*—small moulds of cream with pounded almonds, &c.

—— *à la Chantilly* is made of whites of eggs and cream, with sugar, &c.

—— *à la Celestine*—a mould lined with strawberries and filled with any kind of cream.

—— *à l'Italienne* is made with cream, sugar, eggs, curaçao, dried cherries, candied peel, &c.

—— *à la Flamande* is made of cream, eggs, sugar, arrowroot, madeira, &c.

—— *à la Hollandaise* is made of yolks of eggs and wine, with whipped cream, &c.

—— *à la Bavaroise*—a mould of whipped cream, with flavouring, &c.

Bavarois *aux pommes* is made of stewed apples, with whipped cream and noyau or maraschino.

—— *aux poires* is made in the same way with pears.

—— *aux fruits* is Bavarian cream served with stewed fruit or a syrup of fruit.

—— *aux pistaches*—pounded pistachio nuts and almonds, &c, with whipped cream, coloured with spinach juice; sprinkled with chopped pistachio nuts.

Bavarois *au maizena* is a cream of sugar, milk, maizena and yolks of eggs.

—— *glacé* is iced Bavarian cream.

Crème fouettée *de fraises*, or *Mousse aux fraises*, is whipped strawberries and cream.

—— *aux framboises*—whipped raspberries and cream.

Blanc-manger *au café* is blanc-mange flavoured with coffee; *à la vanille* it is flavoured with vanilla.

—— *aux amandes* is made with pounded almonds, and flavoured with orange-flower water.

Crème *frite à la patissière* is a custard cut in pieces, breadcrumbed and fried.

—— *frite au chocolat*—a chocolate cream cut in pieces, breadcrumbed and fried.

Meringues *à la crème* are meringues filled with whipped cream.

—— *aux fraises* are filled with whipped strawberries and cream.

—— *à la Chantilly* are filled with Chantilly cream.

Petites meringues *aux pistaches* are small meringues sprinkled with chopped pistachio nuts, and filled with whipped cream.

Meringue *à la Parisienne*—a pile of rings of meringue preparation, piped with currant jelly in stripes, the centre filled with cream and garnished with strawberries.

Charlotte *Russe* is a mould lined with finger biscuits, and filled with whipped cream.

—— *Prussienne* is a mould with half an inch of red jelly at the bottom, lined with finger biscuits, and the centre filled with Bavarian cream.

—— *aux fraises*—a mould lined with strawberries, and filled with maraschino cream.

Biscuits *à la crème*—a rich frothy cream, baked in small paper cases.

Parfait *au chocolat* or *au café* is a tall conical mould of chocolate or coffee cream ice.

Glaces *au four* are small pieces of ice, folded in paste and baked.

Glace *meringuée au four* is a mould of any kind of cream ice, covered with a meringue preparation, and browned.

Gâteau *glacé à l'Eloise*—a mould lined with whipped cream, and filled with custard and stewed cherries; iced, and served with custard over it.

Cartouches *de M. de Cupidon*—Love's cartridges—vanilla cream ice in the shape of cartridges, filled with chocolate.

Glace *de Plombières* is an ice of pounded almonds, sugar, cream, eggs, &c. This ice is not put in a mould, and is served with apricot jam.

Bombe *glacée*—a cream of yolks of eggs with syrup, &c., iced in a round "bombe" mould.

M

Granito Romaine is a liquid ice of coffee and syrup, served in little cups.

JELLIES.

Gelée *de pommes*—Apple jelly.
—— *de prunes*—Plum jelly.
—— *d'oranges*—Orange jelly.
—— *de citron*—Lemon jelly.
—— *de cassis*—Black currant jelly.
—— *de cerises*—Cherry jelly.
—— *de framboises*—Raspberry jelly.
—— *de fraises* is jelly coloured red, with whole strawberries in it. If the jelly is flavoured with vanilla, it is called *Gelée de fraises à la vanille*.
—— *de mûres sauvages à la crème*—a mould of blackberry jelly with whipped cream in the centre.
—— *à l'ananas* is pine-apple jelly, with pieces of pineapple in it.
—— *au jus de grenades*—Pomegranate jelly.
—— *à la macédoine de fruits*—whole fruits in a jelly flavoured with maraschino.
—— *au madère*—Wine jelly.
—— *au rhum* is flavoured with rum.
—— *au noyau* is flavoured with noyau.
—— *au marasquin* is flavoured with maraschino.
—— *à la Chartreuse* is flavoured with Chartreuse.

Gelée *au curaçāo* is flavoured with curaçāo.

—— *au ponche* is flavoured with punch.

—— *aù Kirsch* is flavoured with Kirschenwasser.

—— *de Dantzic aux fraises* is flavoured with cherry brandy, and has whole strawberries in it.

—— *de marasquin aux abricots* is flavoured with maraschino, and has pieces of apricots in it.

—— *de noyau aux fruits* is flavoured with noyau, and has pieces of apricots and strawberries, or other fruits, in it.

—— *aux violettes printanières* is made of an infusion of fresh violets in syrup. Jellies of fresh flowers are also made of roses, pinks, jonquils, &c.

—— *à la Bacchante* is made with the juice of green grapes and spinach, champagne, &c.

—— *à la Panachée*—a mould of alternate layers of white and pink jelly.

—— *à la Russe*—a mould of jelly whisked to a froth.

—— *mousseuse à l'eau de vie*—a mould of jelly whipped with brandy.

—— *mousseuse aux oranges*—a mould of orange jelly whisked to a froth.

—— *fouettée aux fruits*— whipped maraschino jelly, with pieces of apricots, cherries, strawberries, &c.

Kiselle is a jelly made of flour with fruit syrup.

SOUFFLÉS.

These may be served in a soufflé dish, or in small paper cases as *Petits soufflés*.

Soufflé *au café* is flavoured with coffee.
— *au chocolat* is flavoured with chocolate.
— *au café vierge* is flavoured with green coffee.
— *au citron* is flavoured with lemon.
— *à la vanille* is flavoured with vanilla.
— *au marasquin* is flavoured with maraschino.
— *aux amandes* is flavoured with pounded almonds.
— *aux macarons* is flavoured with macaroons.
— *aux fleurs d'oranger* is flavoured with candied orange flowers, or orange-flower water.
— *au gingembre* is flavoured with preserved ginger.
— *aux abricots* is made with the addition of stewed apricots. Soufflés are also made with other fruit.
— *à la crème* is made with whipped cream instead of some of the whites of eggs. Baked in small paper cases it is called *Biscuits soufflés à la crème*.
— *au riz* is a rice soufflé flavoured with lemon or vanilla.
— *à la crème de riz* is made with ground rice.
— *au tapioca* is made with tapioca.
— *à la fécule de pommes de terre* is made with potato flour.

Soufflé à la Paysanne—a purée of apples, with a purée of chestnuts with cream over it, and meringue mixture on the top.

—— *glacé au marasquin* is an iced soufflé flavoured with maraschino. Coffee or other flavouring may be substituted for maraschino, and the soufflé named accordingly. Iced in small paper cases it is called *Biscuits glacés au marasquin*, &c.

—— *glacé aux fraises* is an iced strawberry soufflé.

—— *glacé vanille et chocolat*—an iced vanilla soufflé, with chocolate on the top.

—— *glacé au curaçao*—an iced soufflé flavoured with curaçao and covered with a meringue preparation. Iced in small paper cases this is called *Biscuit mousseux glacé en caisse*.

CHAPTER IX.

SAVOURY ENTREMETS OF CHEESE, ETC.

Soufflé *au Parmesan* is a cheese soufflé. As *Petits soufflés* it is served in small paper cases.

Fondue *au Parmesan* is a cheese fondu, baked in a soufflé dish or paper case, or steamed.

—— *à la Napolitaine* has the addition of short pieces of macaroni.

—— *au pâte d'Italie* has the addition of Italian paste. These may all be served in small paper cases as *Petites fondues*.

Petites fondues *en caisse au Stilton* are made with the addition of small dice of Stilton cheese.

Ramequins are made of milk, flour, eggs, grated Parmesan, &c., baked in small paper cases.

—— *à la Raymond* are made with Gruyère cheese, and are baked in small lumps.

—— *à la Sefton*, or *au feuilletage*, are small shapes of puff paste with grated Gruyère and Parmesan cheese.

Ramequins *à la Genevoise*—grated cheese with cream, baked on slices of bread.

Nudeln *au Parmesan* are poached quenelles of butter, flour, milk, eggs, grated Parmesan, &c.

Kluskis *au fromage à la crème* are little poached rolls of a paste of cream cheese, butter, eggs, breadcrumbs, &c.; served with black-butter sauce.

Canapés *au fromage*—dissolved Parmesan on round slices of fried bread.

Croûtes *au fromage*—grated cheese with butter, breadcrumbs, yolks of eggs, &c., spread on pieces of toast and browned.

Brioches *au fromage* are small cakes of brioche paste with grated Parmesan and small dice of Gruyère.

Grugère *au fromage*—butter, grated cheese, flour and eggs, baked with slices of cheese on the top, and glazed.

Crème *de fromage*—a baked cream of grated cheese, eggs and milk.

Petits pains *de fromage* are little cakes of flour, butter and grated cheese.

Fromage *cuit* is toasted cheese.

Tartelettes *à la Sefton* are tartlets of a paste of grated Parmesan, flour, butter, &c., filled with a cheese custard.

Pailles *au Parmesan* are cheese straws.

Pailles *à la Sefton* are cheese straws of puff paste with grated Parmesan.

Diablotins *au Gruyère* are little fried balls, the size of chocolate drops, of a paste of milk, butter, flour, eggs, grated cheese, &c.

Biscuits *au fromage* are cheese biscuits.

—— *à la Diable au fromage* are biscuits spread with cheese, mustard, cayenne, &c., and grilled.

—— *à la Russe*—biscuits spread with chopped parsley, hard-boiled egg and anchovies, and ornamented with the separate ingredients.

Talmouses *à la Saint-Denys* are biscuits of flour, cream curds, cheese, butter and eggs.

Timbale *à la Diable* is a mould of layers of rice with grated Parmesan, &c., with alternately slices of ham and of Gruyère cheese, between the layers of rice. Baked and served with gravy.

Croûtes *au jambon* are ham toasts.

—— *à l'Indienne*—butter, eggs, chopped capers, anchovy, &c., on small pieces of buttered toast.

—— *aux anchois* are small pieces of fried bread spread with anchovy butter or paste. They are sometimes garnished with fillets of anchovy.

Canapés *aux anchois* are round slices of fried

bread with chopped anchovies, capers, yolk and white of egg arranged on them separately in quarters.

Allumettes *d'anchois* are strips of anchovies wrapped in paste and fried.

Anchois *farcis*—anchovies boned, stuffed, dipped in batter and fried.

Rôties à la minime are fillets of anchovies or sardines on oblong pieces of fried bread; served with a sauce of oil, vinegar, &c.

Sardines *au Parmesan* are sardines on buttered strips of toast spread with grated Parmesan.

—— *en papillotes* are boned, stuffed, and served in papers.

Tartines de caviare—Russian caviare spread on small slices of buttered toast.

Canapés à la Prince de Galles—very small rolls filled with chopped ham, anchovies, gherkins and truffles, with oil, vinegar, &c. The top covered with aspic or Mayonnaise sauce.

Macaroni *au gratin*—macaroni with grated cheese and white sauce. Sprinkled with breadcrumbs, Parmesan and melted butter, and baked.

—— *à la crème* is macaroni in a sauce of grated cheese, butter and cream. Garnished with croûtons.

Macaroni à *l'Italienne*—macaroni with grated Parmesan, gravy and melted butter.

—— à *la Napolitaine*—with grated Parmesan, cream, &c.

—— *aux tomates*—with a purée of tomatoes; garnished with croûtons.

—— à *la sauce tomates* is dressed with cream, grated cheese, &c., and covered with tomato sauce.

—— *en timbale*—dressed with butter and grated cheese in a shell of paste, with a paste cover.

Timbale de macaroni à la Florentine is the same with the addition of cream, sugar and vanilla.

Croquettes de macaroni au fromage are croquettes of macaroni with grated Parmesan, Béchamel sauce, &c.; breadcrumbed and fried.

Riz à *l'Indienne* is curried rice.

—— à *la Turque* is rice with melted butter.

—— à *la Milanaise*—a mould of rice boiled in broth, with grated Parmesan, &c.

—— à *l'Espagnole* is served with tomato sauce, grated cheese, &c.; garnished with slices of ham.

—— à *la Florentine*—with chopped onion, curry paste, grated Parmesan, and shrimps or prawns.

Riz à *la Piémontaise*—dry rice with potato pulp, grated Parmesan, &c. Garnished with fillets of anchovies.

—— *a la Polonaise*—served with slices of fried onion, grated ham and cheese.

—— à *la Mustapha*—with melted butter and chopped truffles.

CHAPTER X.

ICES OR GLACES.

At large dinners it is usually the custom to give the names of the ices—cream and water—on the menu; but they are often omitted from it, as they are served after the dessert has been put on the table, and therefore cannot be said to form part of the dinner.

Crème *de thé*—Tea cream ice.
―― *de thé vert*—Green tea cream ice.
―― *de vanille*—Vanilla cream ice.
―― *de ratafias*—Ratafia cream ice.
―― *aux fleurs d'oranger*—Cream ice with infusion of orange flowers.
―― *Bavaroise*—Bavarian cream ice.

The following can be cream or water ices:

Crème, or **eau,** *de café*—Coffee cream or water ice.
―― ―― *de chocolat*—Chocolate cream or water ice.
―― ―― *de noyau*—Noyau cream or water ice.
―― ―― *d'abricots*—Apricot cream or water ice.

Ices.

Crème or eau *de pêches*—Peach cream or water ice.

——— —— *de fraises* — Strawberry cream or water ice.

——— —— *de framboises*—Raspberry cream or water ice.

——— —— *de framboises et groseilles* — Raspberry and currant cream or water ice.

——— —— *de groseilles*—Currant cream or water ice.

——— —— *de cassis* — Black currant cream or water ice.

——— —— *de cerises*—Cherry cream or water ice.

——— —— *de groseilles vertes*—Green gooseberry cream or water ice.

——— —— *de raisins* — Grape cream or water ice.

——— —— *d'ananas*—Pine-apple cream or water ice.

——— —— *de rhubarbe* — Rhubarb cream or water ice.

——— —— *de canneberges*—Cranberry cream or water ice.

——— —— *de citron*—Lemon cream or water ice.

——— —— *d'oranges* — Orange cream or water ice.

——— —— *d'amandes* — Almond cream or water ice.

——— —— *de pistaches*—Pistachio nut cream or water ice.

Crème or **eau** *de marrons*—Chestnut cream or water ice.
—— —— *de gingembre* — Ginger cream or water ice.

In addition to these there are:

Eau *de ponche*—Punch water ice.
—— *de melon*—Melon water ice.
—— *de grenade*—Pomegranate water ice.
—— *d'épine-vinette*—Berberry water ice.
—— *de mille fruits*—Mixed fruit water ice.
—— *de canelle*—Cinnamon water ice.

If orange ice is made of Chinese oranges it is called *de Chinois.*

For water ices fresh fruit is necessary, as preserved fruit can only be used for cream ices.

CHAPTER XI.

SAUCES AND GARNISHES.

SAUCES.

The following are the principal sauces and garnishes which are used in cookery. Many of them have been mentioned in the course of these pages, and as the names frequently convey no idea of their ingredients, a slight description of them is given.

The two chief sauces are *Velouté*—white, and *Espagnole*—brown. Many other sauces are made from these.

Allemande is a thicker form of velouté sauce.

Anchois (Anchovy)—melted-butter sauce with anchovy, &c.

Aurore—Allemande and tomato sauce, with Chili vinegar, &c.

Béarnaise—yolks of eggs, butter, French vinegar, chopped parsley, &c.

Béchamel—Velouté sauce with cream. This is also made without stock if a maigre sauce is required.

Beurre—melted-butter sauce.

Beurre noir—black-butter sauce of browned butter and vinegar. This sauce is usually served with skate or grilled mackerel.

Bigarade is made of oranges with brown sauce.

Blonde—melted-butter sauce made with stock instead of water.

Bordelaise—brown sauce with wine, chopped parsley, &c.

Bourgeoise—stock with French mustard, tarragon, &c.

Bourguignotte—brown sauce with wine, onions, mushrooms and truffles.

Bretonne—brown sauce with onions, &c.

Câpres (Caper)—brown or white sauce, with capers.

Caramel—burnt sugar. It is sometimes made of burnt brandy and sugar.

Cardinal—white sauce coloured with lobster or crayfish butter.

Cazanova—Mayonnaise sauce with yolks of hard-boiled eggs, shred whites of eggs and truffles.

Champignons (Mushroom)—brown or white sauce with purée of mushrooms.

Chateaubriand—brown sauce with Maître d'hôtel sauce.

Chevreuil—Poivrade sauce with wine, Harvey, red currant jelly, &c.

Court-bouillon—wine, or vinegar and water,

butter, vegetables, &c. This sauce is only used in cooking.

Crème—melted-butter sauce with yolks of eggs and cream.

Crevettes (Shrimp) — Cardinal sauce with anchovy, pickled shrimps, &c.

Czarina—brown sauce with sultana raisins, gherkins, &c.

Diable (Devil sauce)—brown gravy with Oude and Harvey sauce, vinegar, &c.

Diplomate—Béchamel sauce flavoured with crayfish.

D'Uxelles—white sauce with chopped ham, mushrooms, parsley, &c.

Estragon (Tarragon)—white stock with Tarragon vinegar, tarragon, &c.

Fenouil (Fennel) — melted-butter sauce with chopped fennel.

Financière—brown sauce with wine, mushroom catsup, &c.

Fines-herbes—brown sauce with chopped mushrooms, shallots and parsley.

Fouettée—sweet whip sauce of yolks of eggs, sugar and wine.

Fumet de gibier—a brown game sauce with onions, wine, &c.

Genevoise—brown sauce with wine, anchovy, chopped parsley, &c. This sauce is generally used for freshwater fish.

Groseilles vertes—green gooseberries with butter, breadcrumbs, &c. For mackerel.

Hollandaise—yolks of eggs and butter with vinegar, &c.

Homard (Lobster)—melted-butter sauce, with lobster spawn and the flesh in small pieces.

Huîtres (Oyster)—oysters in white or brown sauce.

Indienne—tomato sauce with curry paste, anchovy, &c.

Italienne—brown or white sauce with wine, chopped shallots, mushrooms, &c.

Jambon (Ham)—brown sauce with shred ham, butter, chopped shallots, &c.

Jolie fille (Fair maid's)—white chicken sauce with hard-boiled yolks of eggs, breadcrumbs, &c.

Kari—Curry sauce.

Lyonnaise—Portugal onions with tomato sauce, &c.

Maître d'hôtel—Béchamel sauce with chopped parsley, &c. It is also made without stock.

Marinade—vinegar and water with onions carrots, &c.

Marrons (Chestnut)—chestnut flour with brown stock. White chestnut sauce is made of the flour with broth and milk.

Matelote—brown stock with wine, young onions, mushrooms, &c. White matelote sauce is made of broth and wine, with tarragon, &c.

Mayonnaise—a cold sauce of yolks of eggs, oil and vinegar.

Milanaise—grated Parmesan with cream sauce, or with brown sauce and mustard.

Mirepoix—broth and wine with bacon, chopped vegetables, &c.

Moules (Mussel)—a white sauce with anchovy and mussels.

Mousquetaire—oil and Tarragon vinegar, with mustard, shallot, &c.

Moutarde (Mustard) — melted-butter sauce with mustard, Chili vinegar, &c. For herrings.

Napolitaine—brown sauce with Port wine, Harvey sauce, ham, horseradish, currant jelly, &c.

Œufs (Egg)—melted-butter sauce with hard-boiled eggs cut in pieces. Served with haddock and salt cod.

Pauvre homme—vinegar and water with shallots, &c.

Percil (Parsley)—melted-butter sauce with chopped parsley.

Périgueux—brown stock with wine and truffles.

Piquante—brown sauce with vinegar, shallots, &c.

Poivrade—brown sauce with vinegar, anchovy,

ham, onions, &c. White Poivrade sauce is made of white sauce with vinegar, onions, &c.

Portugaise—butter, yolks of eggs and lemon-juice.

Poulette—Allemande sauce with chopped parsley. This is also called *Blanquette*.

Provençale—white wine with tomatoes, chopped capers and mushrooms, garlic, &c.

Raifort (Horseradish)—cream, vinegar and horse-radish.

Ravigote—Maître d'hôtel sauce with Chili vinegar, Harvey and anchovy.

Ravigote verte—white sauce with pounded tarragon, chervil, &c.

Réforme—Poivrade sauce, Port wine, Harvey, currant jelly, &c.

Rémoulade—broth with mushrooms, chopped parsley, mustard, vinegar and garlic. Cold Rémoulade sauce is made of oil with chopped parsley, capers, garlic, &c.

Richelieu is a white game sauce with onions and wine.

Robert—brown stock with chopped Portugal onions, mustard and vinegar.

Russe—a white sauce with horseradish, vinegar, yolks of eggs and cream.

Sainte-Ménehould—milk, butter and flour, with chopped parsley, mushrooms, &c.

Salmis—a brown game sauce with wine, oil, &c.

Sauge (Sage)—stock, vinegar, chopped sage, &c.

Soubise—a purée of onions with cream.

Suprême—a white chicken sauce with wine and cream.

Tartare—Mayonnaise sauce, or oil and vinegar, with mustard, &c.

Tomates (Tomato)—a purée of tomatoes with stock, &c.

Truffes (Truffle)—brown sauce with wine and truffles.

Verte—wine and stock with pounded herbs, yolks of eggs, &c.

Villeroi—white sauce flavoured with mushrooms, &c.

Vin de Madère—brown sauce with Madeira or other wine. It is also a sweet sauce of yolks of eggs, wine, &c.

Vin d'Oporto—Port wine with shallots, Harvey, &c. This sauce is used for wild ducks.

GARNISHES.

Chipolata—small round sausages, pieces of bacon, mushrooms, chestnuts, &c., with brown sauce.

Financière—cock's combs, livers, quenelles, pieces of sweetbread, &c., with brown sauce and wine.

Flamande—carrots, turnips, cabbages and other vegetables, with sausages.

Godard—sweetbreads, quenelles and truffles, with brown sauce.

Jardinière—vegetables cut in shapes, in a light glaze.

Macédoine—vegetables cut in shapes, with brown or white sauce.

Milanaise—strips of macaroni, ham, chicken, truffles, &c., in white sauce with grated Parmesan.

Réforme—shred ham, carrots, truffles and whites of eggs.

Toulouse—Financière garnish made with white instead of brown sauce. This is sometimes called a white Financière garnish.

www.ingramcontent.com/pod-product-compliance
Lightning Source LLC
Chambersburg PA
CBHW020309170426
43202CB00008B/545